The Campus and the City

MAXIMIZING ASSETS AND REDUCING LIABILITIES

A Report and Recommendations by

The Carnegie Commission on Higher Education

DECEMBER 1972

MCGRAW–HILL BOOK COMPANY

New York   St. Louis   San Francisco   Düsseldorf

London   Sydney   Toronto   Mexico   Panama

Johannesburg   Kuala Lumpur   Montreal

New Delhi   Rio de Janeiro   Singapore

This report is issued by the Carnegie Commission on
Higher Education, with headquarters at
1947 Center Street, Berkeley, California 94704.
The views and conclusions expressed in this report
are solely those of the members of the Carnegie Commission
on Higher Education and do not necessarily reflect the
views or opinions of the Carnegie Corporation of New York,
The Carnegie Foundation for the Advancement of Teaching,
or their trustees, officers, directors, or employees.

Library of Congress Cataloging in Publication Data

Carnegie Commission on Higher Education.
The campus and the city.

1. Education, Urban—United States.
2. Municipal universities and colleges—United
States.   3.   Education, Higher—Aims and objectives.
I.   Title.

LB2329.C34   378   72-11696
ISBN 0-07-010058-6

Additional copies of this report may be ordered from
McGraw-Hill Book Company, Hightstown, New Jersey 08520.
The price is $3.95 a copy.

Not a single human achievement was conceived or realized in the bracing atmosphere of steppes, forests or mountain tops. Everything was conceived and realized in the crowded, stinking little cities of Jerusalem, Athens, Florence, Shakespeare's London, Rembrandt's Amsterdam. The villages, the suburbs, are for the dropouts. . . . we will decay, we will decline if we can't make our cities viable. That's where America's destiny will be decided—in the cities.

ERIC HOFFER

Those American universities which happen to be situated in large centers of population are now commonly classified as urban universities. But the term, as used in educational circles, designates something beyond the mere accident of location. The term implies that the university accepts a special obligation to respond to the immediate educational needs of the community in which it is set; that, without compromising the standards appropriate to university instruction and investigation, it plans its offerings with direct reference to these needs; and that within the limits of its resources it is hospitable to all local requests for those intellectual services which a university may legitimately render.

SAMUEL P. CAPEN,

*former Chancellor
University of Buffalo,
at Centennial Convocation
in 1946*

Contents

Foreword

This report, *The Campus and the City,* is intended to give scrutiny to higher education in urban contexts. In it, we consider the special issues and opportunities resulting from the urban setting, and the nature and quantity of higher education resources required to respond appropriately to the needs of the metropolitan area, with special attention to the central city.

Our recommendations cover various aspects of the three significant roles played by colleges and universities in their relationships with the cities and their residents—as educator, as expert, and as major participant in the life of the city. In addition, we make recommendations concerning the organization of higher education resources in each metropolitan area.

Dr. George Nash's case studies of selected urban institutions, which are to be published by McGraw-Hill under the title *The University and the City* as part of the Carnegie Commission's sponsored research report series, provided a valuable background as did also many consultations with Dr. Nash during the preparation of this report. Reports generated from the University of Pittsburgh's University-Urban Interface Project and many helpful discussions with Dr. Robert Brictson, Director of Research Programs, University of Pittsburgh, were also most helpful.

In addition we are especially indebted to those who participated in our advisory conferences: Dr. Theodore Brown, assistant to the president, City College of the City University of New York; Dr. Elizabeth Carrow, director, Speech Pathology Services, Department of Otolaryngology, Baylor College of Medicine; Dr. Warren Cheston, chancellor, University of Illinois, Chicago Circle Campus; Ms. Georgia K. Davis, American City Corporation, Columbia, Maryland; Mr. John Edgerton, Nashville, Tennessee; Dr. Allen Fonoroff, professor of planning, Case Western Reserve University;

Mr. Richard Freeland, assistant to the president, University of Massachusetts Central Office; Dr. Herbert Gans, Center for Policy Research and professor of sociology, Columbia University; Mr. John C. Hetherston, vice-president, coordinated planning, University of Pennsylvania; Dr. Charles Hurst, Jr., president, City College of Chicago, Malcolm X Campus; Mr. Martin Jenkins, Office of Urban Affairs, American Council on Education; Dr. William Rea Keast, Commission on Academic Tenure, Washington, D.C.; Dr. Paul Lazarsfeld, professor of sociology, Columbia University; Dr. Julian Levi, professor of urban studies, University of Chicago; Dr. Raymond Mack, academic vice-president, Northwestern University; Mr. Peter Meyer, program associate, Southern Regional Education Board; Dr. Barry Munitz, vice-president for academic development and coordination, University of Illinois; Dr. Kermit Parsons, dean, School of Architecture, Cornell University; Mr. Clark Shipman, U.S. Office of Education; Dr. Saul Touster, provost, City College of the City University of New York; Dr. Albert C. Van Dusen, secretary of the university, principal investigator, University-Urban Interface Program, University of Pittsburgh; Dr. Robert C. Wood, president, University of Massachusetts; Dr. James W. Woodruff, provost, University of Detroit; Ms. Barbara Wheeler, staff associate, Urban and Ethnic Affairs, Columbia University; and Mr. Larry Williams, National League of Cities, Washington, D.C.

To the many other persons who were consulted and who gave us helpful suggestions, we wish to express our appreciation. We wish also to thank the members of our staff, and particularly Virginia B. Smith, for their work in preparing this report.

Eric Ashby
The Master
Clare College
Cambridge, England

Ralph M. Besse
Partner
Squire, Sanders & Dempsey,
Counsellors at Law

Joseph P. Cosand*
Professor of Education and
Director
Center for Higher Education
University of Michigan

William Friday
President
University of North Carolina

*On leave from the Commission while serving as Deputy Commissioner for Higher Education, U.S. Office of Education, beginning March 1, 1972.

*The Campus
and the City*

1. Major Themes

1 The university was born in the city—Salerno, Bologna, Paris, Prague. But American practice generally has been to establish campuses in small towns and rural areas—this practice reflected the models of Oxford and Cambridge, the Puritan aversion to the "evils" of the city, the "booster" inclinations of small towns, and the choice of agriculturally oriented state legislatures in placing state colleges and universities outside the big cities.

The campuses accepted the practice because they were oriented toward their middle-class students and toward national and world —not local—problems. And the university has been able to prosper in Göttingen as well as in Berlin, in Cambridge as well as in London, and thus also in Iowa City as well as in Chicago.

This dominant American practice has resulted (1) in a deficit in student places in some metropolitan centers and (2) in a lack of widespread campus experience in dealing with city problems until very recent times.

One early reaction of some campuses, as the cities engulfed their once suburban sites, and particularly as the cities then began to decay, was revulsion at the surrounding nightmare and an effort to create a "fortress"[1] like those of the Crusaders in the land of the infidels.

Major exceptions to the historical generalization given above— Temple in Philadelphia, Northeastern in Boston, Wayne State in Detroit, St. Louis University in St. Louis, City College in New York, and the University of Cincinnati, among others—have long been not only *in* but *of* and *for* their cities. After World War II, the Illinois Institute of Technology and the University of Chicago—as two examples—pioneered an approach that was much more construc-

---

[1] See Parsons and Davis (1971).

tive than that of the fortress institutions. But the general ambience of most of American higher education during most of our history has been nonurban. Only Catholic colleges and universities have shown a clear inclination to choose city locations where the populations to which they most appealed have been located. As a consequence, they have had especially close ties to the cities.

But times have changed. American society is now irretrievably an urban civilization. Some of the greatest problems of the day involve the quality of life in the city. Higher education is now reflecting upon and also reflecting these two facts.

2 The campus is now concerned with the city as never before:

- The new urban populism forces attention.
- The interests of faculty members and students are drawn to the agonies of the city.
- Trained intelligence is accustomed to searching out and analyzing new problems as they come along; it can no longer neglect great problems of the age.
- New skills are needed in administering to the city, and the campus seeks to provide the manpower trained in such skills.
- Universalization of access to higher education involves creating places for inner-city youth to seek greater equality of opportunity.
- The city provides contact with reality—new ways to learn.
- The specter of additional confrontations, as at Morningside Heights and Isla Vista, haunts many a board of trustees and many a president.

Thus both out of necessity and out of attraction the campus—both the urban-located and the non-urban-located campus—is drawn to the city.

3 But there is great and understandable hesitancy:

- It is difficult for two very complex entities—the city and the campus—to mesh their actions; they both are pluralistic, even anarchic, constellations of activities.
- Some demands of the city on the campus involve low levels of academic content, and the campus usually is oriented toward higher levels.

- Once involved in a new activity, at whatever level, like hospital service to a ghetto community, the campus can become a hostage to social peace—unable to extricate itself. Moreover, many campuses are trying to disaggregate their activities rather than aggrandize them—simplify, not complicate their functions.

- Attention to the city takes time and money, and both are in short supply.

- The campus is not prepared to respond to emergency calls for instant action, instant results. The community may expect too much —the campus is only a marginal resource in solving urban problems.

- Involvement with the problems of the city enhances conflict on the campus, and between the campus and external groups. The campus is not well prepared to handle confrontations. Nor is it well organized to deal with the new collectivities seeking group advancement —it is more accustomed to dealing with individuals.

- Knowledge-creating institutions need a special insulation from the pressures of political and economic interests, a special protection for their academic functions—and involvement with the city can threaten the needed isolation.

The barriers of additional costs incurred and of greater risks run are substantial.

4 The selection of a course of action thus is difficult. The city and the campus are drawn closer to each other, but they also repel each other.

One principle, however, is clear: the campus for 100 years and more has served agriculture, industry, and the professions, and it cannot now deny service to the new claimants; it should not now or ever base its actions on class bias; it should not now or ever serve only the rich and the powerful, and deny the poor and the weak. The rules it follows should be the same for all. These rules are difficult both to set forth and to apply.

In all service to all elements of society the campus must be cautious and circumspect:

- It cannot do everything everybody wants it to do; some things it cannot do at all.

- It should engage in service only as this relates to its central purposes of teaching and research, to its academic essence.
- It should not do what other institutions of society can do as well or better.
- It must preserve its institutional integrity and essential independence at all costs.
- It must protect itself from domination by any political or economic or social interest group.

The campus has faced the problem of what service to give and under what conditions in numerous times in its history. The difference now is that the issues are more complicated and the pressures, often, more intense.

Service to the city warrants three special cautions:

- Knowledge alone is not enough to solve the problems of urban life.
- The university may not always be the institution best qualified to dispense such knowledge as does exist.
- The campus is better as a "birthplace" for ideas than as a "battlefield" for contending social forces (Meyerson, 1969).

5 The experience of the land-grant universities in assisting agriculture offers no close parallel. The universities did make enormous contributions to agricultural productivity and to the quality of rural life. But they were aided by great breakthroughs in the biological sciences, particularly in genetics. No similar breakthroughs have occurred in the area of the study of urban problems. The social sciences, in particular, are not now prepared to make the same contribution to the city as the biological sciences have made to the rural economy. Nor should the possible future achievements of the social sciences be oversold. Also, in the case of agriculture, the land-grant universities dealt with a few interest groups; the city involves many. And the land grant institutions were usually new institutions performing new functions; while there will be some new urban universities, the new services to the city will mostly come from older institutions slowly taking on new duties.

The campus must find its way without any clear earlier models to follow, although much experience has accumulated: in Chicago with neighborhood relations, in Boston with medical assistance, in California and New York City with open access, in St. Paul and New York State with new types of institutions, in Cleveland with a new mechanism for planning and coordination, in Detroit with continuing education.

6 The campus relates to the city in these several ways:

- In serving urban students

- In training for new occupations related to the needs of the city

- In providing general understanding to students and the public about the nature of urban civilization

- In conducting research through its individual faculty members on urban problems

- In providing service through its faculty members and students to hospitals, schools, and so forth

- In being a neighbor living in the same general environment

- In acting as an employer of local citizens

Most campuses should no longer and can no longer build medieval walls around themselves as self-contained universities or colleges; instead they must create pathways to their many doors. They must be responsive to the city but selective in what they undertake to do. And each campus must look at its own situation and its own environment — and both vary greatly — and decide what it should do.

A few campuses may still be able and still want to isolate themselves from urban affairs; a few more will be able and will want to protect themselves, even though they are not fully isolated, from the pressures of urban problems. But most will either *(a)* expand their interests to include attention to the new urban problems consistent with their prior commitment to disciplinary teaching and research or *(b)* make an all-out commitment to their urban locality specifically and to the problems of the urban setting more generally as their preeminent purpose. Most institutions we believe will come under *(a)*, but an increasing number will also come under *(b)*.

Degree of commitment aside, different institutions will be concerned with different combinations of functions related to the urban environment:

- Open access at the lower-division or the upper-division level or both

- Training of technicians and professional experts

- Applied or basic research
- Service in many forms

One campus, for example, may find its particular emphasis in open access, another in occupational training and applied research, another in professional training and basic research, and another in service.

Both degree of commitment and range of functions will vary enormously.

7   One early step, as each campus contemplates its role, is to look at mutual assets and liabilities.

The campus can be an asset to a community by:

- Creating places for its students
- Training students for work in the community
- Undertaking research, and giving advice and service through its faculty members and students
- Providing cultural and recreational facilities for local residents
- Employing local residents and attracting other employers to the area

When a community seeks a new campus, these are the advantages which are talked about. But there are also some potential liabilities less often realized:

- The campus, particularly when it is large in size, impedes the free flow of community life through it — it blocks traffic and social contacts alike.
- The campus takes property off the tax rolls.
- Many campuses turn their least pleasing aspect — their parking lots — toward the community, making less attractive the adjacent areas.
- Uncertain campus-growth plans may result in deteriorated maintenance of surrounding properties.
- Student "digs" are seldom well maintained.
- Some campuses draw around them "street people," drugs, and crime.

The city, in turn, may create its own liabilities for a campus, particularly a deteriorating physical environment and an unsympathetic or even antagonistic political climate. But the city, on the other hand, provides for members of the academic community a real-life laboratory, cultural facilities like museums and theaters, and places to live and shop.

8 This report makes recommendations primarily in three areas: (1) how to accentuate the assets and reduce the liabilities, (2) how to create more open-access places for students in areas that now have deficits, and (3) how to create mechanisms which will facilitate progress in solving problems. In connection with (3) we suggest:

- Establishment of Metropolitan Higher Education Councils
- Establishment of Metropolitan Educational Opportunity Counseling Centers
- Creation in large urban universities of an administrative position directed toward liaison with the city, and of an advisory council on university-city relationships
- Creation by large cities of the position of liaison officer with postsecondary education
- Campus encouragement of quasi-university agencies or quasi-campus satellites that will relate campus talents and concerns to city needs

  Generally we see a need for more intermediary individuals and institutions between the campus and the city.

9 The goals as we see them for each metropolitan area are:

- Open-access opportunities at some institution of postsecondary education for all students who wish to attend—we set forth the areas with apparent deficits of such opportunities
- One or more area health-education centers or their equivalent
- A Metropolitan Higher Education Council
- A Metropolitan Educational Opportunity Counseling Center, which will help ease growing burdens on colleges and universities to provide extended counseling services

- Agreed-upon plans for campus growth consistent with the development of the area surrounding each campus
- More effective use of any vacancies in any existing higher education institutions, particularly private institutions

The major task, however, is a new concern by each campus to maximize its presence as an asset and minimize its activities as a liability to its surrounding neighborhood and to its metropolitan community, while preserving itself as an academic institution first and foremost.

10 We make two new proposals for programs:

- "Urban-grant" allocations to ten carefully selected universities and colleges to see what they can do with imaginative overall approaches to urban problems. We suggest maximum grants of $10 million over a period of ten years, subject to periodic review at two-year intervals.
- Creation of experimental *learning pavilions* attached to community colleges and to comprehensive colleges directed toward the learning needs of adults through the new technology, discussion groups, and other methods. We suggest that the new program for support of innovative efforts by higher education within HEW be open to such proposals.

11 The time scale for solutions to the growing urban problems is short.

2. The Urban Crisis

On February 28, 1968, in a message to Congress, the President of the United States stated:

Today American cities are in crisis. This clear and urgent warning rises from the decay of the decades—and is amplified from the harsh realities of the present.

Few would take issue with the President's assessment.
Many elements make up the crisis:

- High levels of unemployment and poverty
- Rising rates of crime with city streets increasingly unsafe at night
- Low standards of health care and grossly inadequate health services
- Pockets of severely substandard housing with high density occupation
- Inability of the public educational system to meet the educational needs of the city population, high dropout rates, and continuing problems of illiteracy
- Traffic congestion, rising levels of air and noise pollution, water shortages, and power failures

Many of these are problems throughout the nation, but within the high-density population of urban areas they take on a more intensive and potentially explosive character. Recent years have brought some progress in low-cost housing and some improvement in traffic flows. Successes to date, however, have been overshadowed by inability to cope, on any demonstrable scale, with the major problems of urban America.

While the central city is usually seen as the primary locus of these problems, it does not exist in isolation from the total metropolitan area of which it is a part. It is the interaction of the two areas—

the central city and the suburban ring[1]—that has given rise to the sharpest manifestations of what we now call urban problems. The central city has experienced an erosion of its tax base by the move of businesses from the central city to the surrounding areas, and from the move of high- and middle-income families to suburban residential areas. At the same time, larger concentrations of poor and minority families within the central city have led to increased demands for public services which in turn increase the burdens on central city taxpayers. This continuing upward pressure for greater revenues coupled with the steady erosion of the central city's tax base results in an ever-widening disparity within the central city between the revenues available and the costs of the public services so urgently needed. In a sense, a significant portion of the gain in standard of living available to middle- and high-income families in suburban rings of metropolitan areas has been achieved at the expense of the poor in the central cities who do not have the option of buying a home in the suburbs.

In view of these interactions, and particularly in view of the mismatch between the needs and resources of the central city, it would seem that many of the problems must be solved on a metropolitan regional basis (or even national basis) rather than solely within the central city. But such efforts are handicapped by the fact that the governmental structure of most metropolitan areas can be described as a type of "maze."

The boundaries and jurisdictions of cities, counties, school districts, and special districts typically overlap and conflict in a complex maze. For example, the Chicago Standard Metropolitan Statistical Area has over 1,000 local governments; Philadelphia has over 800. The interdependent activities of people in the metropolis cannot be dealt with comprehensively by any one government. The result is said to be inferior services, economic inefficiences and disparities, and lack of responsiveness to popular control (Marshall, 1972).

[1] It is difficult to use precisely and consistently such terms as "urban" and "city." "Urban" originally applied to the city and is now used in a more general sense, often referring to the entire metropolitan area. And "city" has come to be used in this more general sense also. In this report, we will use "urban" and "city" as the more general terms with the terms "central city" reserved for references to the major city in the metropolitan area, and "suburban" as the remainder of the metropolitan area. We recognize, however, that most metropolitan areas are not this neatly arranged. Central cities may include within their boundaries residential areas more like the suburbs than like the inner city portion of the central cities; and suburbs often include secondary cities which may have some of the features of the central city of the metropolitan area but on a lesser scale.

Donald Canty, in an article calling for a new national urban policy, describes the metropolis as follows:

It is a profligate society, wasteful of its resources, which must some day pay the price. . . .

It is a malfunctioning society. The quality of public services declines even as local taxes continue to rise. . . .

It is a divided society, by class and race. This has been the price of sub-urban exclusivity. The pattern of metropolis is a pattern of de facto apartheid. . . .

The new pattern of metropolis has moved us toward being an unjust society. It is deeply implicated in all of the forms of injustice wrought by poverty and racism . . . (Canty, 1972, p. 32).

Canty believes that a new national urban policy will have to be devised to meet these problems with new agencies designed to replace the present "near-anarchy of the metropolitan pattern" with a sound instrument for governing the metropolity.

Robert Wood has observed that "the metropolitan region is not a political structure but a political system—informal coalitions of local officials, civic leaders, church and university people that form and reform on every issue," and that as "monolithic political machines and cliques of economic notables have disappeared, the university has risen as an increasingly important focal point for bringing coherence and reason to metropolitan affairs" (Wood, 1965, p. 308).

While universities may serve as focal points, solutions to the complex problems of our metropolitan areas lie beyond the power of universities to provide. Solutions must be addressed to:

- Reform in governmental structure of metropolitan areas and major revisions in tax structure
- Substantial improvements in the delivery of health care
- Significant advances in the use of technology designed to deal with population density problems
- General improvement in the level of employment, control of inflation, and economic growth

Solutions such as these require contributions of many types of institutions and agencies both in and out of metropolitan areas. Improvement in the quality of life in our central cities and coping with the complex problems of our metropolitan areas have emerged as high national priorities. While no single set of institutions could be expected to make significant progress by itself in responding to these priorities, both the complexity and severity of the problems make it the responsibility of every type of institution to determine what it can best contribute to the solution. Colleges and universities are seen as having potential for aiding in the solution. It is the purpose of this report to examine the various roles of American colleges and universities, to suggest those ways in which they might positively affect the urban situation, and to caution against those college and university actions that are likely to exacerbate the situation. This type of examination is fraught with difficulties; urban-located colleges and universities may well become a part of the problem for which they are seeking a solution. At the same time, the many elements of the urban problem act upon the urban college and university leading to new stresses for higher education in the city.

3. Higher Education and the City

The troubles that beset American higher education today are sharpened by the crisis of American cities. Pressures created by urban problems reinforce the demands from within our colleges and universities for reassessment of higher education's priorities and functions. The challenge is to forge a new relationship between the campus and the city that will both aid the city and revitalize urban higher education.

This task is complicated by past legacies and present forces that propel the constituents in different, sometimes opposite directions:

- Demands for new urban-oriented services and programs come at a time when many colleges and universities are facing a period of financial stringency.

- Dependence on political units and private donors for resources makes institutions reluctant to become closely involved directly in highly controversial city problems. But the demands for involvement, coming from groups both within and without our colleges and universities seem to be growing.

- While rising proportions of urban youth are both economically and educationally disadvantaged, many of our major urban-located colleges and universities have increased both their student charges and admission standards over the last several decades.

- While planners and community members call for removal of the university's medieval walls and for a campus completely open to the public, concern for security has led some urban-located institutions to seek ways to close their campuses to outsiders.

- Massive size of many urban institutions of higher education, and more recently, campus unrest, have lead to greater drains on costly city services at the same time that urban-located institutions have expanded and may

13

continue to expand and thereby remove more property from the tax rolls of the city and reduce property available for residential and other purposes.

- To preserve academic freedom, many inside the campus insist that the university or college must remain aloof from direct involvement in social problems, but others insist that at this time in history educational institutions must serve as agents of change directly aiding in the solution of today's problems.

- Institutions of higher education, historically oriented to white middle-class clientele, find it difficult to cope with the needs and demands of the economically and culturally disadvantaged, and of the blacks and other ethnic groups.

This pattern of tangential and sometimes opposing forces will complicate the development of a more effective relationship between city and campus. The problem of achieving such a relationship while at the same time strengthening our colleges and universities will be the focus of this report. We will consider primarily those institutions located in the inner cities and metropolitan areas, but we will also direct attention to the special responsibilities of colleges and universities, wherever located, to deal with a great central force in American life—the American city. Naturally, both the type of institution and its location will have a major impact on the manner in which these special responsibilities are perceived and discharged.

The city also has an important stake in the future of our urban educational institutions. Indeed, many see the possibilities for revitalization of the city tied very closely to the renewed development of higher education in the city. Henry T. Heald, former president of the Ford Foundation, suggested that:

The University is one of the few immovable islands in a sea of urban change. The American city is perhaps the most fluid, large social unit in the history of mankind. Urban families move on the average of once every five years. Business and industry relocate in response to a variety of fluctuating economic pressures. Neighborhoods rise and neighborhoods fall. Today's boulevards are tomorrow's slums. . . . As a permanent institution of strength the university serves as an anchor in the city's desperate effort to arrest its disintegration and achieve a new stability (in Klotsche, 1960, p. 67).

Colleges and universities also increasingly recognize that their fate and the fate of the cities are inextricably linked. The call for a new and massive commitment of higher education to the problems of the city is strong both from within the academic community and from within the city. There are some within the academic community, however, who urge that universities resist offering many of the services sought from them and who believe that it is folly for institutions, some of which are presently in serious financial difficulty, to take on more functions that would add further burdens. Others believe that many colleges and universities are not equipped to undertake the tasks now sought by the public and that their real contribution can only be made by renewing their original mission rather than redefining it. Among these is Irving Kristol, who has asserted:

The collective responsibility of the university is education. That is its original mission, that is its original purpose, that is the only thing it can claim expertise or authority for. To return to this original purpose with renewed seriousness, would be an action at once radical and constructive (Kristol, 1970, p. 237).

While the debate continues concerning the wisdom of responding to the call, universities and colleges across the nation are instituting various research and public service programs directed to the problems of the cities, are adding courses and degree programs with urban focuses to their curricular offerings, and are cataloging their various educational, public service, and research activities that have urban orientations in order to demonstrate to the public the strength of their commitment.

In 1968, the American Association of State Colleges and Universities began to issue the *Urban Affairs Newsletter,* listing various types of urban projects underway at more than 100 state colleges and universities. The list has included tutorial projects, inner-city teacher training programs, children's recreational programs, community leadership workshops, literacy projects, storefront learning centers, police training, and a large number of workshops and conferences on community problems. Not all higher education's "urban activities" are new, but the rhetoric surrounding them has changed. Continuing education, which has been with us in one form or another for well over a century, is now considered an important "urban activity" if it takes place in a metropolitan area. On the other hand, many college and university "urban activities" represent marked additions to the institution's functions. And in some cases these additional functions have been undertaken without adequately relating the new to the existing functions, and with a sense of evangelism that makes pleas for caution and careful assessment of institutional resources in terms of the task appear heretical.

Harold Enarson, president of Cleveland State University, explained higher education's rush to develop an urban mission in this way:

We bring to the task of community uplift Boyscout eagerness, secular zeal, and liberal compassion. As True Believers in the Baconian notion of Knowledge as Social Power we are not afraid to dream the impossible dream of social salvation in race relations, political salvation in community relations, and economic salvation in development. We bring as well the intolerable weight of a guilty conscience, for have we not rejected blacks in the name of high standards, trained Peace Corps workers in the arts of community development for Brazil but not Harlem, and done research in Calcutta and Pakistan to the neglect of Watts and Hough (Enarson, 1969, pp. 129–130).

Zeal is not enough. While the rhetoric concerning the need for a new commitment by higher education to the city is simple enough, the reality of developing helpful educational research and public service programs that are within the capacity of the colleges and universities is complex indeed. Much of the rhetoric seems to imply that the phrase "needs of the city" has a generally recognized definition. Unfortunately, it is a chameleon-like concept. To those interested in equality of educational opportunity, the educational resources of the inner-city become a central focus; to those concerned with transportation and waste disposal problems, the focus shifts to the entire metropolitan area including the outer suburban ring; to those concerned with the impact of the institution on its environs, the "city" may be narrowed to the immediate neighborhood; and, to those concerned with the development of professional leaders, the city may mean its formal government. When "community" is related to a major research university, the community broadens to the nation or the world.

Regardless of which concept of city or community is involved, those seeking to translate the institution's commitment into action must decide, for their purposes, who determines the needs and the priorities among them. Who, also, speaks for the city? Are expressed *wants* of groups within the cities the same as *needs?* And should the same voices within the city be equally important for the guidance of all types of institutions—for the research university as well as the community college, for the private and public colleges alike?

Moreover, it is not always clear what part of the college or university is expected to provide the service in question—is it the institution as such, its students, or perhaps its faculty members acting as individuals.

Thus the relationship between the "city and campus" is not a single relationship between two clearly identified entities but rather a whole series of relationships with the identity of the participants shifting somewhat from one relationship to another, and from time to time.

We believe, however, that certain of these relationships carry obligations which higher education has not yet adequately met and opportunities it has not yet fully realized.

- Increasing demand for higher education and the development of new educational clienteles with large concentrations in our cities are sometimes poorly matched by the existing higher education resources in many of our cities.

- Shifts in the structure of jobs in professions, social services, and government provide new opportunities for joint participation in the development of revised educational programs for new manpower needs.

- Wise choice of urban public service activities and research projects could make the city a highly effective laboratory for higher education while at the same time making positive contributions to the life of the city.

- Ways must be found to facilitate appropriate use of higher education resources by the urban student.

- Cities' higher education resources must be organized in a way which will enhance their overall value to the city.

- Each college and university must learn to assess its impacts—physical and environmental, economic, social and cultural—on the life of the city.

4. The Urban University and the Urban College

The communication value of terms such as "urban commitment," "university-urban interface," "urban mission" and "urban university" has been seriously eroded by their changing use over time and their present use to cover a very wide range of activities and types of institutions. The lack of commonality of definition handicaps meaningful discussion. To some, "urban commitment" refers only to admission and education of minority students; to others it means social action. And, in the recent past, its most common translation was a commitment to urban renewal. Concern with transportation, pollution, and poverty are also generally considered urban-oriented activities. For some, the existence of an urban research center is sufficient to testify to a university's urban commitment, while others believe urban orientation requires a complex of services including day care centers and legal and health aid for students and the city's poor.

As suggested above, there has been some change in the use of the term "urban university" over time. It is this change in meaning that makes it possible to reconcile the frequently stated view that university concern with urban problems is a phenomenon of the last decade[1] with the fact that the Association of Urban Universities (AUU) was established over a half a century ago. The 14 universities[2] that joined together in 1914 identified matters of special interest to urban universities as, among others, adult education, community service, and university extension. The original 14

[1] See, for instance, Jenkins (1971b, p. 1).

[2] The University of Akron, Boston University, University of Cincinnati, City College of New York, Hunter College, University of Louisville, New York University, Northwestern University, University of Pennsylvania, University of Pittsburgh, State University of New York at Buffalo, Temple University, University of Toledo, Washington University.

universities were about evenly divided between private universities located in cities and municipal universities. The municipal universities relied heavily on the municipal government for financial support and had, in most instances, originally been established expressly for the purpose of making higher education accessible to academically able residents of the city at a cost to the student which would permit the poor as well as the rich to obtain a college education. Some examples:

- In 1819, the City of Cincinnati established a college with nominal fees for residents of the city. This was the first municipal university in the United States.

- In 1847, the Free Academy was established by New York City to provide higher education for young men of promise without regard to race, creed, or financial ability. The Free Academy later became the City College of the City University of New York.

- In 1884, Dr. Russell H. Conwell, established in Philadelphia what was to become Temple University. He conceived of Temple as dedicated to the ideal of educational opportunity for the able and deserving students of limited means.

The proceedings of the AUU's annual conferences indicate that early attention of the group focused on concerns of the university in its educational role. One entire meeting was devoted to the use of field work within the curriculum, to the problems of accrediting field work, and to organizational matters between the university and the agencies in which the fieldwork was to be accomplished. A subsequent meeting was concerned with how urban universities could improve the quality of the cities' elementary and secondary schools. And adult education was the subject for one of these early conferences.

Over the decades since the establishment of the AUU, the concept and role of urban institutions have added several dimensions. By the middle of the twentieth century, certain major private universities, while continuing to select their student bodies nationally, showed their urban concerns in other ways. Research efforts were directed to problems of the city, and the universities participated either directly or indirectly in urban renewal and redevelopment projects in their immediate environs. Boston University established a Metro Center to study various aspects of the interaction between the city and the campus. Urban-located medical schools, such as in

Boston, Chicago, and Philadelphia established health care services in connection with their teaching functions.

In more recent years, certain established institutions have added urban-oriented functions and some multicampus state institutions have developed new campuses in major metropolitan areas and have attempted to relate their development and mission to their urban environment. For certain of these institutions, such as the Boston campus of the University of Massachusetts and Minnesota Metropolitan State College, the urban environment has acted as a primary influence on the total concept of the college.

While the educational needs in the mid-nineteenth century were viewed in terms of additional low-tuition places for students with clearly demonstrated academic ability, the need today is frequently expressed in terms of providing adequate student spaces and financial support not only for highly able students but also for students who have not given clear traditional evidence of academic qualification but who aspire to education beyond high school. The City University of New York's move to open admissions responded to this new definition of educational need, and other colleges have adjusted admission requirements for at least a portion of their student body to accommodate such students. It is likely, however, that the two-year community college with its policy of open admissions will make the major response to low-income students who have not clearly demonstrated academic ability. In addition to meeting urban educational needs, the basic concept of the community college, which usually includes public funding from local sources, control by local boards, and a commitment to serve both full- and part-time students of all ages, would seem to make it particularly suited to carrying out many urban-oriented missions.

Thus, there are many types of institutions of higher education which could be considered, in varying degrees, "urban colleges or universities" under different definitions of that term. An institution that is fully oriented toward urban concerns would have developed its educational, research, and service programs to be responsive to urban needs, would have organized its decision-making mechanisms to work well with those of the metropolitan area and would conduct itself in its corporate role in a way that makes its presence in the city an asset rather than a potential liability.

It is doubtful that any institution has such a total urban orientation. But an institution that takes its responsibility to urban society in general and to its own urban locale in particular as a dominant force in determining institutional objectives and allocating institutional funds, can be considered an urban university or college even though its particular combination of urban activities includes only a portion of those activities generally identified as urban activities. No one institution can respond to the total range of needs of a major metropolitan area. The functions are not only diverse, but some are occasionally incompatible with others. Even if an institution wished to provide the total complex of functions, it would often be unwise to attempt to do so. Nor is it necessary, since each metropolitan area has a variety of higher education resources within it.

Each institution must define and examine its own urban activities[3] in the context of the combined activities of colleges and universities in the metropolitan area, the special needs of the area, and its own general institutional mission. Such an examination should include the various roles of the institution:

- Role as educator[4]
- Role as creator of knowledge[5]
- Role as provider of public services[6]
- Role as corporate member of the community[7]

[3] For an aid to self-studies of urban activities see Jenkins (1971a).

[4] Discussed in Chapters 6, 7, 8, 9, 10, and 11.

[5] Discussed in Chapter 12.

[6] Discussed in Chapter 13.

[7] Discussed in Chapter 14.

5. Role as Educator

The most traditional and central of higher education's many functions is education of an enrolled student body. In developing their educational programs, urban-oriented colleges and universities should consider the special educational needs of an urban population including:

- The availability of student spaces for residents of metropolitan areas
- The creation of programs designed to provide skilled and professional manpower needed for urban management and development
- The development of curricula and institutional support activities responsive to the needs of urban students
- Effective use of the rich educational resources (museums, theaters, parks, etc.) of the city in their own educational activities
- The cooperative use of city agencies and industry to provide effective education and service

College and university leaders who wish to define their educational functions in terms of an urban mission, must become students of their own areas. They must learn the quantity and nature of total postsecondary resources in the area. They must learn the characteristics of the population. And in the light of these they must consider their own admissions policies and curricular offerings. Some states' education agencies or city agencies have undertaken studies of the supply and demand of higher education resources within metropolitan areas. The recent study of higher education in the Boston Metropolitan Area is an excellent example of such a study.[1] In Minneapolis–St. Paul, the Citizens' League recently

---

[1] See Massachusetts Board of Education (1971).

undertook a study of need for new higher education institutions in that area. Occasionally, individual researchers provide excellent information on higher education—in particular, metropolitan areas such as that provided for Illinois, including detail on Chicago education resources, by Doris Holleb (1972). In such studies have not been undertaken, this should be an initial step in the development of metropolitan educational resources designed to meet metropolitan needs.

6. Access to Higher Education in Metropolitan Areas

There is no good substitute for intensive study of each metropolitan area, but it is possible from examination of gross comparative data of higher education resources in metropolitan areas to make preliminary and tentative findings of deficiencies, thus identifying those areas that have the greatest need for further careful and detailed analysis.

TOTAL HIGHER EDUCATION PLACES Appendixes A and B provide information on student spaces in colleges and universities compared with population in each of the 99 metropolitan areas having more than 100,000 residents. In 1970, the combined population of these 99 areas constituted 57 percent of the total population of the nation, and total student enrollment in the colleges and universities in these areas accounted for approximately 61 percent of the total national enrollment. In the nation as a whole, in 1970, about 25 percent of all enrollment was in private institutions, but in the 99 metropolitan areas, 30 percent of enrollment was in private institutions. Over 70 percent of total private collegiate enrollment in the United States is in private colleges and universities located in metropolitan areas, while less than 60 percent of public institution enrollment is in metropolitan areas.

We have compared enrollment with the total population rather than with 18- to 21-year-olds because we believe that higher education should be available to people over their lifetimes, not just to the 18- to 21-year-olds. Similarly, we have used total enrollment rather than degree credit enrollment because we believe that the adequacy of resources should be considered in the light of general educational demands, not just the demands of those who wish to take traditional degree programs. Although incomplete, this analysis provides one important set of measures of adequacy of the higher education resources of a city.

Access to higher education by residents of different metropolitan areas will be affected by the availability of student spaces. In 1970 the Lansing, Michigan, metropolitan area had almost 14 student places per 100 population, while the Fort Lauderdale–Hollywood area had only 1.3 spaces per 100 population. Among major metropolitan areas (those with population over 1 million), Indianapolis, with 2.1 places per 100, had the lowest ratio.

There are some regional differences. As shown in Table 1, metropolitan regions in the New England area had the highest average percentage with the Western regions at almost as high a figure. The Southeast, North Midwest, and Central regions had substantially lower levels.

We believe, in the absence of unusual circumstances, that any metropolitan area that has fewer than 2.5 student spaces per 100 population is unlikely to be able to meet the educational needs of its residents. On the basis of 1970 data, the following metropolitan areas fall in this category:

Metropolitan area	Student spaces per 100 population
Canton, Ohio	1.52
Davenport–Rock Island–Moline, Iowa	2.47
Fort Lauderdale–Hollywood, Florida	1.30
Gary–Hammond–East Chicago, Indiana	2.43
Indianapolis, Indiana	2.12
Jacksonville, Florida	2.32
Kansas City, Missouri	2.35
Little Rock–North Little Rock, Arkansas	1.89
Louisville, Kentucky	1.93
Mobile, Alabama	2.28
Norfolk-Portsmouth, Virginia	1.85
Paterson-Clifton-Passaic, New Jersey	2.23
Tulsa, Oklahoma	1.69

NOTE: The location of these areas is shown in Map 1.

Of these metropolitan areas, Indianapolis, Kansas City, and Paterson-Clifton-Passaic are areas with one million or more population. On the basis of our general data, these areas would seem to be deficient in higher education resources. More detailed studies might, of course, refute this preliminary finding. Differences in the

Region	Number of metropolitan areas in region	Average percent	Median percent	Range
New England	7			
Total		6.44	5.92	4.72–10.55
Central city		12.60	11.29	5.90–19.97
Suburban		2.99	3.26	0.55–4.87
North Atlantic	20			
Total		4.08	3.66	2.23–8.83
Central city		8.21	6.98	0.00–20.29
Suburban		2.34	2.57	0.37–6.43
Southeast	22			
Total		3.47	3.41	1.30–7.51
Central city		7.30	6.18	2.39–17.46
Suburban		0.75	0.44	0.00–3.47
North Midwest	17			
Total		4.16	3.38	1.52–13.83
Central city		8.32	6.55	3.06–39.82
Suburban		1.57	1.00	0.00–5.64
Central	6			
Total		3.48	3.56	2.35–4.90
Central city		6.35	5.50	3.12–10.39
Suburban		1.03	1.24	0.00–1.50
Southwest and Mountain	13			
Total		4.52	4.64	1.69–8.41
Central city		5.51	3.87	1.78–14.64
Suburban		2.97	0.46	0.00–12.04
West	14			
Total		5.68	5.22	3.01–8.40
Central city		10.81	10.23	3.40–18.44
Suburban		3.10	2.88	0.00–6.60

SOURCE: Compiled by Carnegie Commission staff.

composition of the population in terms of age, or in the capacity of existing institutions to expand, or in the proximity of the area to an area with more than adequate facilities combined with excellent interarea transportation systems, or in the extensive use of postsecondary institutions other than the colleges and universities reflected in our data could affect the need for new institutions. In some urban areas as the result of actions since 1970, the latest year for which we have comprehensive enrollment data, these deficiencies may have been greatly alleviated. But where serious deficiencies still exist in terms of the guidelines set forth above, we suggest the need for immediate action to increase availability of postsecondary education.

We recommend that appropriate state and local agencies take steps to improve availability of student places in colleges and universities in those areas which now have less than 2.5 places available per 100 population.

On the basis of 1970 data, as noted above, this would require action in the 13 areas shown in Map 1.

Metropolitan areas that have a ratio of student places to population between 2.5 and 3.5 might be considered as having a marginal deficiency in total available resources. Metropolitan areas that fall in this category are:

Metropolitan area	Ratio of student places to population
Allentown-Bethlehem-Easton, Pennsylvania	3.39
Atlanta, Georgia	3.37
Beaumont–Port Arthur–Orange, Texas	3.44
Birmingham, Alabama	2.74
Charleston, South Carolina	2.85
Chattanooga, Tennessee	2.77
Chicago, Illinois	3.38
Cincinnati, Ohio	3.16
Cleveland, Ohio	2.73
Dallas, Texas	3.28
El Paso, Texas	3.12
Flint, Michigan	2.73
Grand Rapids, Michigan	2.98
Harrisburg, Pennsylvania	3.24
Houston, Texas	3.22
Jersey City, New Jersey	2.84
Lancaster, Pennsylvania	3.19

Metropolitan area	Ratio of student places to population
Nashville, Tennessee	2.54
New Orleans, Louisiana	3.44
Pittsburgh, Pennsylvania	3.18
San Antonio, Texas	3.03
St. Louis, Missouri	3.27
Tacoma, Washington	3.01
Utica-Rome, New York	2.78
Wilkes-Barre-Hazleton, Pennsylvania	2.81
Youngstown-Warren, Ohio	2.99

NOTE: The location of these areas is shown in Map 2.

While the deficiencies in these 26 areas are not so marked as those for the 13 areas shown in Map 1. They nonetheless may be a cause for some concern.

We recommend that appropriate state and local agencies undertake an evaluation of the adequacy of the number of higher education student places in the 26 areas listed above and shown in Map 2.

We recognize that the ratios used in the preceding analysis are only rough measures of availability of higher education to residents of a metropolitan area. Areas which appear to have adequate spaces may in fact have deficiencies because of factors not reflected in this data. Enrollment at colleges and universities in metropolitan areas, for example, includes many from outside the area. Exact figures on this are not available, but the proportion of out-of-state students enrolled in institutions in each metropolitan area suggests an upper limit to the proportion of student spaces in a metropolitan area now used by students from that area. Of course, these figures are less useful when more than one state is included in the boundaries of the metropolitan area.

As shown in column 2 of Appendix B, several metropolitan regions have a high proportion of out-of-state enrollment. Almost half of Denver's enrollment is out of state, and 44 percent of Nashville's enrollment comes from out of state. Several metropolitan areas have approximately one-third of their enrollment from out of state: New Orleans, 31 percent; Boston, 33 percent; Springfield–

MAP 1: *Metropolitan areas deficient in total student places*

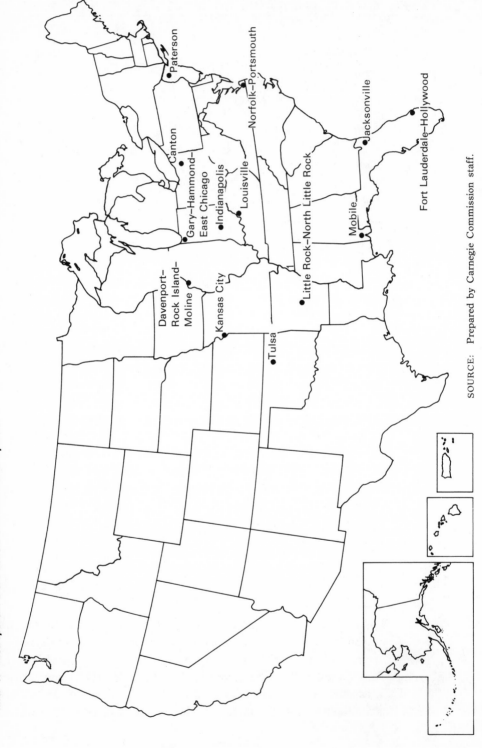

Paterson

Norfolk–Portsmouth

Jacksonville

Fort Lauderdale–Hollywood

Canton

Gary–Hammond–
East Chicago

Indianapolis

Louisville

Little Rock–North Little Rock

Mobile

Davenport–
Rock Island–
Moline

Kansas City

Tulsa

SOURCE: Prepared by Carnegie Commission staff.

MAP 2: *Metropolitan areas marginally deficient in total student places*

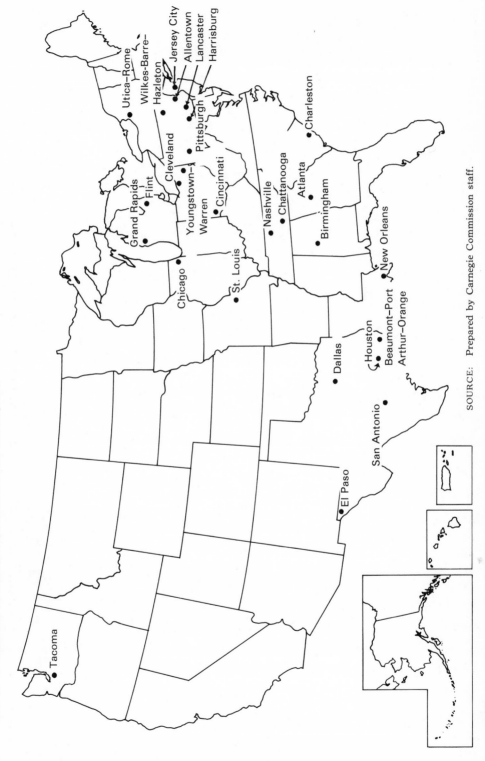

SOURCE: Prepared by Carnegie Commission staff.

MAP 3: *Metropolitan areas adequate in total student places*

SOURCE: Prepared by Carnegie Commission staff.

Chicopee–Holyoke, 36 percent; Flint, 31 percent; Trenton, 31 percent; Greensboro–Winston-Salem–High Point, 30 percent; Dayton, 37 percent; Charleston, 35 percent. With the exception of Denver, these areas are in the East and are in states with a heavy proportion of private colleges which tend to draw their students from a broader geographic area.

We are not suggesting that enrollment in colleges and universities in metropolitan areas should be limited to residents of the area, but clearly variations in proportions of out-of-state enrollment must be considered along with total student spaces in estimating potential deficiencies in total higher education resources in the various areas.

For those metropolitan areas located entirely within the boundaries of one state, modification of the ratio of student spaces to population by out-of-state enrollment provides a somewhat more accurate measure of adequacy of resources for the metropolitan population. On this basis, 6 of the 26 metropolitan areas identified as marginally deficient—Flint, Michigan; Cleveland, Ohio; New Orleans, Louisiana; Tacoma, Washington; Utica-Rome, New York; Youngstown-Warren, Ohio—would be moved to the deficient category.

Two cities would move from a preliminary finding of adequacy to one of deficiency: Denver, Colorado; and Knoxville, Tennessee. And an additional group of cities that might otherwise have been considered adequate in their resources would move to the category of marginal deficiency. They are: Dayton, Ohio; Greensboro–Winston-Salem–High Point, North Carolina; Greenville, South Carolina; Miami, Florida; Milwaukee, Wisconsin; Newark, New Jersey; Orlando, Florida; Peoria, Illinois; Philadelphia, Pennsylvania; and Tampa–St. Petersburg, Florida.

On the basis of the modified categories, out of the 99 metropolitan areas, the ratio of enrollment to population suggests deficiencies of higher education resources in 21 metropolitan areas, and marginal deficiencies in an additional 28 metropolitan areas, leaving 50 metropolitan areas with an initial finding of adequacy of total higher education resources.

Because it was not possible to modify the enrollment ratios for all areas for nonresident enrollment and also because the most recently available student migration figures are for 1968, we have not included the above cities in our recommendations about deficiency and marginal deficiency areas. We think, however, that the analysis presented above indicates that differences in migration patterns may well mask a deficiency in terms of the residents of particular metropolitan areas.

We recommend that careful studies be made in the areas noted above to determine whether present patterns of nonresident enrollment correspond closely with those of 1968 and, if so, to take whatever steps are necessary to expand facilities for higher education.

BALANCE WITHIN METROPOL-ITAN AREAS

Growth in population in metropolitan areas is occurring primarily in suburban regions rather than in the central cities. But the resources for higher education are largely concentrated in the central cities. As shown in Appendix B, in all but six metropolitan areas in 1970, the ratio of student places to population was much higher in the central cities than in suburban areas. In 20 metropolitan areas there were no colleges or universities outside the central city, and in another 26 there was less than one place per hundred outside the central city. Although the income level of many inhabitants of suburban areas would make it more possible for young people to go away to college, nonetheless there will be some who will need educational resources close to home. The imbalance which exists in most of the metropolitan areas, with the resources in the central city and the residents in the suburban areas, contributes to the already complicated transportation problems of the metropolitan regions.

The imbalances are not limited to location but also extend to type of institution. In the ratio of student spaces to population we have used enrollment as the measure of student spaces. While this provides the best readily available approximation of student spaces, it is most accurate for this purpose when each institution is fully utilizing its capacity. A recent study, however, indicates that, in 1970–71, there were approximately 110,000 unfilled freshman places (Peterson, 1972, p. 22). Over half of these places were in private colleges and universities. Thus, while it would seem that there would be an inadequacy of student spaces in some metropolitan areas, there might at the same time be a surplus of student spaces of a type for which students do not have effective demand. Both economic and ability barriers could prevent students from utilizing available student spaces.

An examination of Appendix C, which provides information on patterns of higher education resources within metropolitan areas, shows how this situation could occur. In the central city, as contrasted with the suburban ring of the metropolitan area, many of those aspiring to college may be both economically and educationally disadvantaged. In 1968 there were twice as many families below the poverty level in the central cities than there were in the suburban ring (U.S. Bureau of the Census, 1970, p. 70). And in the decade between 1959 and 1968, the gap between median incomes of families in the central city and the suburban ring widened. In 1959, the median income in central cities was 89 percent of that in the suburban ring; by 1968 the percentage had dropped to 84 percent (ibid., p. 25). Recent federal legislation for student financial aid, if fully funded, may help to reduce economic barriers, and several states have recently expanded their student-aid programs. This will make more places available to more students at more institutions.

Many high school graduates of central city schools in major metropolitan areas are ill equipped to enroll directly in college-level work. In her recent study of colleges and the urban poor, Doris Holleb cites the fact that juniors attending high schools in Chicago, with the exception of a small number of high schools, were performing at a level far below the national average. In fact, juniors at 20 of the city's high schools could not demonstrate ability to read at the eighth-grade level (Holleb, 1972, p. 25ff.).

Lack of adequate financial resources and the necessity of living at home or working while in school force many high school graduates either to seek their higher education experience in their cities of residence or to forgo it. For at least a considerable portion of the high school graduates within the central city, this requires that there be available, as a part of the higher education resources of the city, open-admissions institutions. An examination of Appendix C suggests the mismatch which exists in several cities between the need for certain types of institutions within the central city and the institutions that actually exist there. Some central cities appear to have adequate total student spaces but lack sufficient open-access spaces.

Washington, D.C., has only recently added open-access institutions to its higher education resources and, as indicated in Appendix C, a major portion of available student spaces in that city continues to be in selective-admissions universities. It is difficult to determine just by an examination of Appendix C which metropolitan areas are lacking in open-access spaces. We do know that most two-year public colleges have an open-admissions policy, but some public comprehensive colleges and universities also operate on an open-admissions basis. Furthermore, some private institutions are quite flexible in their admission practices, but their tuition charges, unless accompanied by adequate financial aids for students, are a barrier to access.

We believe that at least one-third of the spaces in the central city's colleges should be available on an open-admissions basis.[1] As recommended in earlier reports, we believe that two-year community colleges are the most suitable institutions to operate under an open-admissions policy, but we also believe and have recommended that more selective institutions provide for some portion of their enrollment (perhaps 10 percent) on the basis of flexible admissions standards. For central cities with less than one-third open-admissions places, at least a prima facie case can be made for deficiencies in open-admissions spaces. It should be stressed that identification of such cities is only for the purpose of urging the city to undertake a more thorough study of its open-access spaces. Clearly, a final determination of whether or not it has adequate spaces of this type requires substantially more information than that supplied in Appendix C. On initial examination, all but 17 of the central cities in the 99 metropolitan areas have less than one-third of their spaces in open-access low-tuition institutions. More detailed studies would be required of admission policies of the institutions and of student-aid programs available to students to determine whether barriers to access have been overcome in institutions other than public community colleges. For example, Federal City College is not a two-year community college, but it operates on an open-admissions basis. Certain other four-year public institutions also operate on an open-admissions basis, although in these insti-

---

[1] Across the nation as a whole approximately 28 percent of all enrollment is presently in community colleges, but in those states with fully developed community college systems, almost half of all enrollment is in community colleges. Experience in these states with a high percent of the age group attending college suggests that we might expect as many as 70 percent of the high school graduates to enroll in college. Since selective-admission institutions rarely admit below the upper half or third of the class, this would leave a substantial number of students requiring places in less selective institutions. In addition, a considerable number of students, though eligible for admission to selective institutions for financial reasons, or because they wish to remain at home, will wish to enroll in a conveniently located community college. In view of these factors, we believe that one-third of total student places in community colleges or other open-admissions institutions is a desirable target.

tutions it is necessary to distinguish between the formal standards for admission and the informal admission practices. Also, with creative use of combined federal, state, and institutional sources of student financial aid, it is possible for some private colleges to remove effectively the financial barriers for large proportions of their students. Excellent examples of this are the Central YMCA College of Chicago and Berea College in Kentucky. This is not possible in the absence of effective state and federal student-aid programs.

The Commission is not recommending that every central city have within it sufficient public two-year colleges to accommodate one-third of its college enrollment. We are recommending, rather, that state planning agencies, through metropolitan task forces, study in depth the higher education resources available in their central cities to find ways to insure that at least one out of every three undergraduate student spaces in the central city be available on an open-admissions basis with either low tuition or effective student financial-aid programs.

In prior reports *Quality and Equality* and *The Capitol and the Campus,* we have made recommendations for effective student-aid programs at both the federal and state level. We will not repeat those here, but we do wish to stress that the particular types of mismatches of supply and demand in many of the central cities do not lend themselves to simple solutions. In fact, in central cities that have a large proportion of private institutions, the rapid development of new public two-year colleges would, to some extent, increase the surplus of spaces at the private colleges. On the other hand, this result may be inevitable if no ways are found to utilize the surplus spaces for the types of students whose educational demands have not been met. Thus, before development of new institutions, careful consideration should be given to expansion of student-aid programs and cost-of-education supplements to private institutions in order to use surplus student spaces. Some institutions in the central city with selective admissions may wish to reconsider their educational missions to determine whether it would be possible for them to modify their admissions policies.

The President's Committee on the Future University of Massachusetts (1971) was particularly sensitive to the problem of access. In its report, after reviewing the composition of the University of Massachusetts' student body and the educational needs of Massachusetts, the committee recommended that "the university adopt new admissions criteria in order to maximize the accessibility of the institution to" minority students, low-income students, older students, women, and transfer students, "without jeopardizing its commitment to excellence." To implement this policy the committee recommended that "the majority of students should be admitted according to a formula based solely on ranking in high school class or grades. A substantial minority should be admitted according to individualized determination based on such factors as interview, judgment as to exceptional talents and potential, and recommendations. A process of individualized determination will be as important for large numbers of older students as it is for many low-income students."

This deficiency of appropriate space within metropolitan areas has also been highlighted in a recent study by Warren W. Willingham. Willingham studied the availability of free-access higher education, using the following criteria for his definition of free access: The college charge must be no more than $400 in annual tuition, at least one-third of the freshman class must be composed of students who graduated in the lower half of their high school class, and the college must be within 45 minutes commuting time from the student's home. On the basis of this definition, Willingham found that:

Of the 29 metropolitan areas that have a population of more than 1 million, Atlanta, Boston, Buffalo, Cincinnati, Detroit, and Paterson-Clifton-Passaic do not have one free-access college located within their city limits. In eight additional metropolitan areas, less than one-third of the central city population lives within commuting distance of a free-access college. In another nine metropolitan areas, less than a third of the fringe population is covered. Since any one of these conditions must be regarded as a serious urban problem, it is reasonable to conclude that 23 of the 29 largest cities of the country have a major deficiency in the accessibility of higher education. Equally disturbing is the number of metropolitan areas that have no free-access college at all (as of 1968). The Census Bureau defined 228 standard metropolitan statistical areas, most of which had a population of 100,000 or more. In 102 metropolitan areas the principal city had no free-access colleges (Willingham, 1970, pp. 30–31).

It is possible to argue with Willingham's definition of free access. But his findings and our own tentative findings suggest that both economic and educational barriers still prevent many residents of central cities from obtaining education beyond high school.

A further examination of Appendix C indicates that many central cities, even though they may have adequate entry-level places for low-income students in community colleges, have not provided the type of student spaces in which they would be able to complete their undergraduate education. For example, 87 percent of Bakersfield, California, college enrollment is in a public community college, but only 8 percent of the enrollment is in a comprehensive four-year college. This situation might change dramatically in the next few years, since a public comprehensive college has recently been established. In Oxnard-Ventura, California, the pattern is similar: 88 percent of the enrollment is in a two-year public college and 13 percent in private liberal arts colleges. In three Florida areas, Fort Lauderdale–Hollywood, Jacksonville, and Miami, 59 to 89 percent of the enrollment is in public community colleges, and the areas lack any other type of public institution. And in Indianapolis, 17 percent of the enrollment is in a public two-year college, and 46 percent of the enrollment is in professional and specialized institutions without any public comprehensive college.

Of course, in some of these areas private institutions do offer appropriate transfer spaces to students completing the two-year community-college program. This is true, however, only to the extent that there are adequate financial aid programs for low-income students, and that the private institutions have appropriate admissions policies for transfer students.

And the presence of adequate four-year institutions to complement the community colleges is not sufficient by itself. Many students who have earned their A.A. at two-year community colleges, with the intention of transferring to four-year institutions, are often frustrated at the time of transfer to find that much of their work cannot be credited toward a baccalaureate degree or that, even though credited, deficiencies must be made up which will lengthen the time required to complete their bachelor's program.[2] While the problem of articulation between community colleges and four-year or upper-level colleges is not limited to metropolitan areas, it seems that, particularly in metropolitan areas, much could be done to alleviate the problem. In a subsequent section of this report, we will be making recommendations concerning organization within metropolitan areas to improve the utilization of higher education resources.

[2] For a discussion of the problems of articulation between two-year and four-year colleges, see Willingham (1972).

Of the areas that are seriously deficient in total student spaces (including those that have deficiences when nonresident enrollment is taken into account), the following 20 appear to be seriously deficient in open-admissions places in their central cities on the basis of information available to us at this time:

- Atlanta, Georgia
- Beaumont–Port Arthur–Orange, Texas
- Cincinnati, Ohio
- Denver, Colorado
- El Paso, Texas
- Greensboro–Winston-Salem–High Point, North Carolina
- Houston, Texas
- Jersey City, New Jersey
- Knoxville, Tennessee
- Lancaster, Pennsylvania
- Little Rock–North Little Rock, Arkansas
- Louisville, Kentucky
- Nashville, Tennessee
- Newark, New Jersey
- Paterson-Clifton-Passaic, New Jersey
- Peoria, Illinois
- Philadelphia, Pennsylvania
- Pittsburgh, Pennsylvania
- Tulsa, Oklahoma
- Youngstown-Warren, Ohio

Although not so seriously deficient, our analysis suggests some deficiency in open-admissions spaces in nine other central cities, and marginal deficiency in an additional nine central cities. These 18 central cities are also in metropolitan areas that have deficiency or marginal deficiency in total student spaces. The deficient cities are:

- Charleston, South Carolina
- Chattanooga, Tennessee
- Chicago, Illinois

- Dayton, Ohio

- Indianapolis, Indiana

- Kansas City, Missouri

- Mobile, Alabama

- New Orleans, Louisiana

- Norfolk-Portsmouth, Virginia

Central cities with marginal deficiency are:

- Allentown-Bethlehem-Easton, Pennsylvania

- Birmingham, Alabama

- Cleveland, Ohio

- Dallas, Texas

- Harrisburg, Pennsylvania

- Milwaukee, Wisconsin

- Orlando, Florida

- St. Louis, Missouri

- Wilkes-Barre–Hazleton, Pennsylvania

Because all these areas are also deficient or marginally deficient in total student places, the particular deficiency for open-admissions places can perhaps best be corrected through addition of new institutions.

There are also, however, several metropolitan areas that appear to have adequate total student spaces for present population but inadequate open-admissions spaces in their central cities. Table 2 lists these cities.

In our report *New Students and New Places* (Carnegie Commission, 1971*b*), based on enrollment estimates to 1980, we called for establishment of some 175 to 235 additional two-year community colleges with from 80 to 125 of these colleges to be established in metropolitan areas with populations in excess of 500,000. Specific recommendations from that report for these major metropolitan areas are reproduced in Appendix E. In that appendix we have revised certain of the estimates based on more recent data. Based on the analysis for the present report, we also believe that of the new 15 to 20 two-year colleges should be established in those metropolitan areas of 100,000 to 500,000 population identified as currently deficient in both total and open-access student places.

Seriously dificient	Deficient	Marginally deficient
Akron, Ohio	Albany-Schenectady-Troy, N.Y.	Bridgeport, Conn.
Albuquerque, N.M.	Anaheim–Santa Ana–Garden Grove, Calif.	Los Angeles–Long Beach, Calif.
Baltimore, Md.	Buffalo, N.Y.	Phoenix, Ariz.
Binghamton, N.Y.	Detroit, Mich.	Portland, Ore.
Boston, Mass.	Fort Worth, Tex.	San Diego, Calif.
Columbia, S.C.	Honolulu, Hawaii	San Francisco–Oakland, Calif.
Columbus, Ohio	Kansas City, Mo.	Seattle–Everett, Wash.
Hartford, Conn.	Lansing, Mich.	Springfield–Chicopee–Holyoke, Mass.
Memphis, Tenn.	New Haven, Conn.	
Minneapolis, Minn.	Rochester, N.Y.	
Oklahoma City, Okla.	San Jose, Calif.	
Omaha, Nebr.	Syracuse, N.Y.	
Providence-Pawtucket-Warwick, R.I.	Trenton, N.J.	
Richmond, Va.	Tucson, Ariz.	
Salt Lake City, Utah	Worcester, Mass.	
Toledo, Ohio		
Washington, D.C.		
Wichita, Kans.		
Wilmington, Del.		

In metropolitan areas with a currently satisfactory ratio of student places to population but a deficiency of open-admission places, any need for new facilities resulting from expected growth in total enrollment should probably be met first with the development of open-admissions institutions. A more desirable first step in these areas, however, would be to reevaluate admissions policies at existing institutions in the area as well as considering granting public subsidies to private institutions which could expand availability of open-admissions places.

In our report *The Capitol and the Campus,* we made several recommendations designed to utilize more fully the resources of private higher education:

The Commission recommends that states establish a program of tuition grants for both public and private institutions to be awarded to students on the basis of financial need. Only after establishment of a tuition grants program should states consider raising tuition levels at public institutions. To avoid upward pressures on private tuition from such grants, states would need to set a maximum tuition grant (Carnegie Commission, 1971*a*, p. 86).

The Commission also recommends that states enter into agreements, or make grants, for the purpose of continuing certain educational programs at private institutions (for example, Florida and Wisconsin grants to private medical schools). These should be selected after consideration of special manpower needs, evaluation of existing student places for these programs in public institutions, and the relative costs of expanding public capacity or supporting and expanding private programs (ibid., p. 97).

The Commission also recommends that those states that do not already have programs enabling private institutions to borrow construction funds through a state-created bond-issuing corporation take steps to develop such agencies if the private institutions can demonstrate the need for them (idem.).

For those few states in which the above recommendations prove inadequate, and this might be the situation in states which rely heavily on private universities and colleges, the Commission recommends that each resident student be given cost-of-education vouchers which would entitle any private institutions selected by the student to receive a state payment increasing gradually each year up to an amount equal to one-third of the subsidy granted by the state for students at the same levels attending comparable public institutions (ibid., p. 98).

We think these recommendations have particular significance for making the best use of all colleges and universities in metropolitan regions.

We add here the recommendation that private colleges reexamine their admission policies to determine whether expansion of open-admission or flexible-admission student places in their institutions would be compatible with their particular educational missions.

In our report *New Students and New Places,* we estimated that 80 to 105 comprehensive colleges would be needed by 1980, with 60 to 70 in urban areas with population in excess of 500,000.

On the basis of our analysis for this present report, we estimate that another 9 of the 80 to 105 comprehensive colleges should be located in metropolitan areas with populations between 100,000 and 500,000 even after fuller utilization of the resources of private institutions.

Metropolitan areas must also have adequate facilities for professional training. Each planning authority should analyze professional training facilities within its area and determine whether new facilities are required. In our report *Higher Education and the Nation's Health* (Carnegie Commission, 1970*b*), we estimated the need in metropolitan areas for new health manpower education centers. In that report we recommended establishment of 33 area health education centers in 28 of the metropolitan areas considered in this report. We also recommended establishment of six university health science centers in metropolitan areas. (The specific recommendations are summarized in Carnegie Commission, 1970*b*.)

The findings and recommendations in this report are based on 1970 enrollment figures. It is quite possible that steps have already been taken in some metropolitan areas to expand available open-admissions institutions and comprehensive colleges. In those instances, the deficiencies mentioned here may already be alleviated to a large extent. But, if this has not occurred, it is hoped that the preliminary findings of deficiencies mentioned in this report will stimulate planning authorities in those areas to undertake an immediate reassessment of their educational resources.

Making adequate numbers of student spaces available and removing barriers to enrollment are necessary first steps to providing for the educational needs of residents of the metropolitan areas. They are not, however, sufficient by themselves. What happens to the student after he is admitted to the institution is as important as making his admission possible.

7. Access Is Not Enough

In our report *A Chance to Learn*, we said:

As higher education increases its efforts to overcome deprivation of educational opportunity, evidence grows that these efforts require a transformation of higher education's own often unbalanced academic and cultural environment (Carnegie Commission, 1970a, p. 15).

Many central-city students have the academic skills that permit them to adjust quite comfortably to a traditional college program. There are many, however, who do not. Doris Holleb states:

The greatest, single hurdle for the graduates of urban, lower-class high schools is the quality of the education with which they customarily emerge and their shaky mastery of skills and concepts essential to further learning. The failure of many urban schools to reach and teach even their most talented students, much less those of average ability, is a nationwide problem of the highest priority. . . . Whatever the causes, it is plain that a high proportion of the graduates of urban high schools, segregated by class and race, are foredoomed to academic failure in conventional colleges without considerable special help. Without such help, an open-door admissions policy is little more than a revolving door, leading only to a repetition of earlier frustration and not to higher education (Holleb, 1972, pp. 80-81).

The logical response to such a problem is improvement of elementary and secondary schools. In a subsequent report we will consider ways in which higher education can work more closely with elementary and secondary education for the purpose of improving education at those levels. But higher education cannot wait for this improvement to occur. Thousands of such underprepared students are already seeking admission to higher education, and thousands more are already enrolled. At least in the short run, a part of the problem of developmental education—the development of basic skills—must be accomplished at the higher education level.

In our report *A Chance to Learn,* we made some recommendations addressed to how higher education might meet this problem. We proposed the adoption of a "foundation year" in which students are given intensive counseling and wide latitude to find a program that fits their interests and needs. This foundation year could be tailored to more rapid, less rapid, or customary progress, to a degree depending on the past training and ability of the individual student. We recommended "initiation of programs for an individualized foundation year available on an optional basis to all interested students." We reaffirm that recommendation here and stress further that the foundation year, in both community colleges and four-year colleges, be individually tailored to both the student's educational goals and to his specific combination of competencies at the time of admission to the college.

Both for the development of these individualized foundation years and also for personal and financial reasons, low-income and educationally disadvantaged students require substantially greater student services than other types of students. Open-admissions colleges and colleges that have programs for the educationally and economically disadvantaged have found that tutorial programs, financial aid counseling, and both special educational and vocational services are essential for the students. Beyond this, such colleges find a need to provide for their students certain services that have never been available at more conventional institutions or that conventional institutions are now beginning to think of dropping because they are so expensive. For example, students from low-income families have substantial needs for free health services. Day-care services for children of working parents who are students or employees of the institution also seem desirable. And some colleges that have made a special point of serving low-income students have found that legal aid must be made available at least on an emergency or first-interview basis to their students.

Increasingly, students seeking higher education in an urban setting will be part-time students (Peterson, 1972, pp. 8–9, 24–25). Financial-aid policies, and scheduling of classes and library and student service hours should be scrutinized to be certain they are not established for a traditional full-time student rather than for part-time students. Institutions, such as the Central YMCA Community College and the new Minnesota Metropolitan State College that are consciously directing their program to urban students, have found that adjustments in both of these areas are essential to meet the needs of their students.

In many colleges and universities, the usual approach is to have a fairly high student-faculty ratio in the beginning years, gradually declining to a quite low ratio in the advanced levels of instruction. For disadvantaged students, and perhaps for many students, this arrangement is far from satisfactory. In the SEEK programs at CUNY, an effort was made to restrict classes to 15 students. Typically, developmental programs utilize classes that are much smaller than those in the standard program. Furthermore, faculty members who are willing to devote their major efforts to teaching activities are sought as participants for such programs. In many institutions the reward structure is such that the faculty may not at any given moment have a large enough number of such members, and those they have may find it difficult to obtain the promotions and other rewards available to others within the institution.

The task of adapting to student bodies with different educational needs is not a neatly circumscribed task with an easy solution. Case studies showing the many elements involved are available for some institutions (Nash, forthcoming). And a recent publication gives one faculty member's view of the metamorphosis at CCNY (Kriegel, 1972).

While the subtle changes in ambience, image, and interrelationships that must accompany an institution's determination to serve the educational needs of significant portions of the urban clientele are not fully known, it is clear that colleges that seek to serve large numbers of lower-income minority students and part-time working students must:

- Provide highly individualized educational programs at least for a "foundation" year
- Make available a greater range of student services including adequate financial-aid counseling, educational and vocational counseling, health services, and, at least, initial or emergency personal counseling and health services
- Devote a greater portion of their resources to the entry-level students
- Modify their institutional reward structure to provide adequate rewards for commitment and excellence in teaching

The Commission recommends that colleges enrolling large numbers of disadvantaged or minority students review their institutional programs in each of the above four areas to determine if they are designed to meet the educational needs of the students involved.

While four-year colleges have enrolled low-income and minority students, the major burden has fallen on community colleges. Unfortunately, community colleges have often been given inadequate resources to provide appropriate student services and adequate developmental programs for these students.

The Commission recommends that state financing authorities and local agencies review their policies for funding community colleges to determine whether adequate funds are being made available for this segment of higher education with its difficult and important tasks.

8. New Directions for Place and Time

Colleges and universities are increasingly recognizing that not all instruction must take place on the campus. They can serve more students and at greater convenience to the students by dispersing certain types of educational programs throughout the metropolitan area. Classes can be held in industrial plants, in schoolrooms, in residential areas, or in libraries. Some universities are experimenting with closed-circuit television so that the instructor can remain on the campus while his presentation is transmitted to groups in various parts of the city.

Among the nine units of the City Colleges of Chicago is a TV college. And the programs of Chicago's City Colleges are conducted at over 100 instructional sites including church basements, storefronts, warehouses, and private homes (Palola & Oswald, 1972, p. 23).

The President's Committee on the Future University of Massachusetts was sensitive to the possibilities of geographic dispersion of educational programs. Plans had already been developed for location of the Boston campus of the University of Massachusetts at Columbia Point. But after restuding the situation, the committee recommended:

In order to promote the physical accessibility of learning and the possibility of community service, we recommend that the plans for the Columbia Point campus be modified. Columbia Point should be developed not as the sole University of Massachusetts/Boston, but as the nucleus of an urban university system which is dispersed throughout the Boston area.

Most of the University's Boston program should be based at Columbia Point, but many should be available in other parts of the community, too. The present facility at 100 Arlington Street downtown should be retained. In addition, UMB should offer classes using the facilities of high schools, public agencies, businesses, and other colleges; contract with corporations, public agencies, museums, hospitals, and other outside agencies who offer programs partially at these locations; develop course offerings which utilize new technological possibilities; . . . (President's Committee on the Future University of Massachusetts, 1971, p. S-5).

Patterns of work and residence in urban areas, transportation concerns, and the need for better utilization of physical facilities all underline the growing desirability of dispersing some of the university's educational programs throughout the urban area. New technological developments will aid greatly in accomplishing this dispersal.

The Commission recommends that urban campuses, in appropriate instances, offer certain portions of their programs in off-campus facilities—at industrial plants, in business and government offices, and at public libraries and schoolrooms in residential areas.

LEARNING PAVILIONS While geographic dispersion will make education more readily accessible to many, there are also substantial benefits to bringing learners to the campus, to make the campuses visible and attractive educational resources for residents of the community.

For this purpose we recommend consideration of the establishment of *learning pavilions* at community colleges and comprehensive colleges located in central cities.

Learning pavilions would provide a home base for adult learners, technological aids for independent study, basic-education programs, and general-education discussion groups. Many colleges are already providing these educational services through extension or continuing-education programs. But we believe that coordination and expansion of such programs under the aegis of a new vehicle, such as the proposed learning pavilions, will increase their visibility and communicate a new sense of educational mission.

Colleges are also experimenting with scheduling approaches that will make higher education available to many who have other commitments during the traditional class schedules. For example, the California State College and University system is experimenting with a weekend college. Increasingly, colleges concerned with extending education in the inner city are moving to 12- to 14-hour schedules for availability of college personnel as well as for class scheduling.

9. Community Colleges and Commuter Colleges

In earlier reports[1] and in Chapter 6 of this report, we have placed great reliance on two-year public colleges to expand equality of educational opportunities. In Chapter 7 we have pointed out several adaptations which any college that is attempting to serve the special educational needs of the low-income and minority residents of the urban area must make. Many of those adaptations apply particularly to community colleges in urban areas, but there are also other special aspects of urban community colleges that require consideration.

Community colleges hold great promise for urban areas. In fact, in terms of education and service, they might well be considered the urban parallel to the land-grant institutions. Unfortunately, they have not yet always lived up to their promise. Community colleges have been assigned some of the most difficult tasks in higher education but have not received in sufficient measure either the human or capital resources necessary to accomplish these tasks. Development of a clear-cut educational mission is still impeded at many community colleges by their being at a somewhat "awkward" age. On the one hand, certain matters of administration, certification, compensation of faculty, and modes of instruction seem too often to bear an unnecessary similarity to secondary public schools. On the other hand, the concern of some colleges for academic status has led them to emulate four-year institutions in certain other—not always the most desirable—respects. Some community colleges, however, such as Malcolm X in Chicago, have made excellent progress in creating an educational program adapted to the needs of their urban clientele. Several of CUNY's colleges under the new open-admissions policy are also adapting their educational programs in response to an increasingly heterogeneous student body.

[1] Carnegie Commission on Higher Education (June 1970d, October 1971b).

While a community college in a rural area may serve primarily as a feeder institution offering the first two years of a baccalaureate program, we believe that the urban setting and an urban student body will encourage and permit urban community colleges to develop truly distinctive educational missions and to use educational processes particularly suited to those missions. In an urban area the potential student body is large enough to permit several community colleges to be established with some degree of specialization among the colleges. For example, one college might specialize in paramedical professional training while another would build a program around the various types of social-service activities. To some degree this type of specialization already occurs in certain urban areas, but in others there is a tendency to herd all students together onto one massive campus.

In their recent study, Palola and Oswald examined six multiunit metropolitan community colleges in terms of their effectiveness in responding to inner-city needs. Although Palola found some notable exceptions of successful inner-city programs, he concluded that:

Familiar barriers to the fulfillment of the missions and roles of inner-city community colleges still persist: a lack of commitment to the concept of developmental education, a level of financial support inadequate for the critical program and service needs of this institution, and continued rigidity of district-wide organizational arrangements even in light of differing environmental settings (Palola & Oswald, 1972, p. 101).

In some instances by design and in others by default, community colleges presently have major responsibility for attempting to make up for deficiencies in elementary- and secondary-school education. They have used a variety of approaches for these programs, but as yet no definitive research has provided guidance on which approaches are the most successful. We believe that one of the most valuable contributions that could be made by community colleges is to engage in systematic experiments of remedial and developmental programs that include adequate evaluative techniques to provide the much needed answers. If research expertise is not available among the college personnel, researchers should be sought outside the campus to work with the faculty in the design and evaluation of the experiments.

Community colleges with well-developed remedial programs might also consider contracting with high schools in the area to provide such education to high school students who seem to have ceased making academic progress in their high school studies. Students who are doing poorly in their high school work might not be aided by spending another year in high school but may find that an early transfer to a community college program designed particularly for improving their basic academic skills may provide the change of setting and increased attention that would improve their learning capacity.

Early admission might also be arranged for students who have particular vocational interests and who do not wish to take further academic work at the high school. In the past, the early admission procedure has been reserved primarily for students who are academically gifted. We believe, particularly in the case of urban community colleges, that under the circumstances just described, early admission to a community college or contractual arrangements for a part of the student's work might be particularly advantageous to students who have little desire or motivation to continue in the high school setting.

With the emphasis in community colleges on career education, we believe that the urban community college is in an ideal position to develop cooperative-education programs. In the past, community colleges have seemed rather slow to experiment with such approaches. In 1970–71 the United States Office of Education Cooperative Education Program gave grants of $1.5 million to 74 institutions. Only 15 of these grants went to two-year colleges ("The Cooperative Education Program," 1971, p. 36).

In view of the various considerations discussed above some new facilities and procedures are required.

We recommend that urban community colleges, in order to serve more fully their urban clientele, give careful consideration to the following:

1. Establishment of multiple campuses in a metropolitan area rather than concentration of all students on one campus, and the development of some specialization of educational missions among the various campuses

2. Systematic experimentation and evaluation of remedial and developmental programs

3. Possible early admission of urban high school students requiring remedial work or seeking immediate entry into vocational training programs

The community colleges and some four-year colleges in urban areas are commuter colleges. But many of these colleges are not designed physically or educationally with the particular needs of the commuter in mind. Scheduling of both educational and extramural activities should recognize commuter needs. Special facilities such as lockers and study areas should be made available to commuters. Many commuters might feel more of an attachment to the institution if there were adequate lounge and study areas which they could utilize on a regular basis and where they could form relationships with other commuting students who use the same areas. Cafeterias and other food services should also be planned with the commuter in mind.

The Commission recommends that commuter institutions make available lockers, study and lounge areas, and other physical facilities designed to meet the special needs of commuters, and that scheduling of educational programs and activities be undertaken with the commuter in mind.

Commuter institutions, particularly urban community colleges, may have accepted too completely their commuter character. Effectiveness of some of the educational programs may be hampered by the complete lack of any residential facilities. During periods when intensive study is needed, commuter students may have no alternative but to return to their homes, in many cases an environment in which it is difficult to study. Some of the inadequacies inherent in a totally commuter college might be alleviated by the provision of flexible residential facilities on the model of the student hostel. Students wishing to spend a night, a weekend or a somewhat longer period at the college could obtain low-cost housing at the hostel. The hostel could also be used for intensive educational programs organized by the college, and it might also provide some of the space required by students during the day seeking a quiet place to study. The availability of such facilities would expand the curricular and program flexibility of the commuter college. It would also be possible to use these facilities for community purposes such as residential conferences.[2]

[2] This proposal is discussed in Corcoran (1972).

10. Need for New Types of Urban Institutions

Urban educational needs will be met in part by the creation of some additional community colleges and comprehensive four-year colleges, and by the expansion and modification of existing urban institutions. But the need to provide flexibility in postsecondary educational experiences will undoubtedly require establishment of some new types of institutions. Addition of these new institutions will effectively expand the options available to those seeking some form of higher education. They can be responsive in part to the improvements in the structure of postsecondary education which we called for in our report *Less Time, More Options*. In that report we recommended:

. . . that alternative avenues by which students can earn degrees or complete a major portion of their work for a degree be expanded to increase accessibility of higher education for those to whom it is now unavailable because of work schedules, geographic location, or responsibilities in the home (Carnegie Commission, 1970c, p. 20).

Some of the alternative avenues proposed in that report, such as the "open university" or certain types of external degree programs, could as easily be established in nonurban as in urban areas. Other new institutional types are, however, particularly well adapted to utilize the resources of the city and to meet the needs of city students. For these new institutions, the metropolitan areas of our nation provide both a substantial concentration of demand and an excellent setting in which to develop the special characteristics of the institutions.

MINNESOTA METROPOLITAN STATE COLLEGE In May 1971, the Minnesota legislature authorized establishment of the Minnesota Metropolitan State College (MMSC). This experimental college, which is being planned simultaneously with its be-

55

ginning operation, is breaking new ground in its recognition that each individual learner has unique educational needs and in its interaction with the life of the city. MMSC has several features which distinguish it from other American colleges and universities:

- It is designed especially for adults in an urban area.

- It has no campus of its own—rather the city is its campus.

- It has no terms, i.e., no semesters or quarters; rather, it operates on a continual basis.

- Most of its faculty members are paid not for time and effort expended in teaching students but for competencies which students actually acquire through their tutelage.

- Each student, in consultation with his adviser, establishes his own educational goals in five competency areas:
  - (1) Basic learning and communications
  - (2) Civic involvement
  - (3) Confidence in vocation, profession, or career
  - (4) Leisure and recreation
  - (5) Personal growth and assessment

- An individualized instructional program to accomplish the student's goals is designed by the student and his adviser. The program typically includes a variety of learning experiences such as independent study, participation in various types of community events, group learning activities, and practical experience such as an internship or on-the-job training.

- The degree is earned on the basis of demonstrated competencies rather than on accumulation of credits.

A college such as this not only makes use of underutilized resources in the city, it also aids the student to begin viewing the city as a learning resource and helps him to organize his life in the city so that many aspects of it become effective learning experiences. MMSC's President Sweet, recently described the educational philosophy of the college in this way:

It is our conviction that colleges tend to teach students to be dependent upon the college instead of teaching them how to function as effective members of the community as a whole. . . . The goal of MMSC, on the other hand, is to offer an education which teaches students how to make cities work—not how to make colleges work. . . . Without a campus, and, with the faculty drawn directly from the cities, MMSC provides the students with a new appreciation of urban life—not as it too often is, but as it can become. The function of the college is not to create a college community, but to support the creation of a total community where all citizens can live a good life (Sweet, 1972).

UNIVERSITIES WITHOUT WALLS In 1970 the University Without Walls program was established. Twenty-one public and private institutions throughout the nation are presently members of the UWW consortium.[1] The University Without Walls project at each of the participating institutions differs somewhat from the other UWW projects. But all have certain elements in common: they seek to build highly individualized and flexible programs of learning, making use of new and largely untapped resources for teaching and learning; in most, the role of the instructor is redefined as facilitater and coparticipant in the planning and design of the student's learning experience. As noted above, these are also central features of the Minnesota Metropolitan State College. Three UWW institutions[2] have incorporated the basic philosophy of UWW into their entire educational program, and all of their students are now considered UWW students. The other institutions operate a UWW project separate from their regular college programs. UWW projects typically use variable time frames, and individual educational programs are developed by the student and his adviser to meet educational objectives defined by the student in consultation with the adviser. Some of the UWW projects continue to translate the learning experiences into credits earned while others are attempting to break away from the credit-hour formula. Some have adopted the learning contract in which a student specifies objectives he hopes to achieve, and how and when he hopes to accomplish them.

The UWW programs are not without their critics. Although the underlying philosophy has much to commend it for older and/or highly self-motivated students, the lack of structure and limitless freedom of choice may actually deter learning for those who are immature or lack self-discipline. Moreover, application of the principle

---

[1] The 21 institutions are: The University of Minnesota, the University of Massachusetts, Antioch College, New College at Sarasota, Shaw University, the University of South Carolina, Roger Williams College, Bard College, Chicago State University, Goddard College, Howard University, Friends World College, Northeastern Illinois University, Stephens College, Loretto Heights College, Staten Island Community College, Skidmore College, Morgan State College, New York University, Westminster College, and Westminster College branch at Berkeley, California.

[2] Goddard, New College, and Friends World College.

that learning is not confined to the classroom, but may occur any-where in an endless variety of circumstances has led to questionable awards of degrees or credits in some instances.[3] In traditional colleges, there has always been some part of a student's credit which was granted on the basis of his experience in the classroom or other instructional activity rather than on demonstrated results of that experience. It is this unmeasured (and some would argue, unmeasurable) element that many faculty members implicitly use to justify granting credit on the sole basis of satisfactory perfor-mance of an examination. And, some types of field activity, not always carefully supervised or integrated into an educational frame-work, have earned credit in some institutions. More recently, this concept has been expanded to permit credit for a variety of activi-ties. For some students in some UWW programs, this element has been carried to the extreme—credit is granted for the experience, occasionally retroactively, without any effort to determine the educational results of the experience. If quality is to be maintained in educational programs based on the principle underlying the UWW programs, it will be necessary to make considerable pro-gress in the development of useful assessment and competency evaluation techniques.

The major experimental elements of UWW programs are well matched to the educational needs of some students, particularly older students, and the basic concept of educational facilitation rather than educational supply is well matched to the rich concen-tration of varied educational resources in urban areas. It would seem desirable for more urban-located colleges to experiment with this approach but to also assess carefully the basis on which edu-cational gains are certified.

COLLEGE FOR HUMAN SERVICES The College for Human Services in New York has developed a new kind of professional curriculum in the human services, emphasiz-ing the closest possible relationship between classroom and field work, and creating an interdisciplinary college-level curriculum based on concepts in the social sciences and humanities. Within the structure of an educational institution this program effectively combines educational and service concepts. The change in curric-

---

[3] For examples, see London (1972).

ular approach was so great that Audrey Cohn, the founder of the college, believed that it was not possible to establish it through curricular reform in existing institutions.

This model transfers to the paraprofessional and professional fields elements of the guild apprentice model combined with features of our formal educational model for preparing professionals. The student very early becomes a paid junior member of the profession, and the formal education portion of the program is designed to have an immediate relevancy that is difficult to achieve in those situations in which formal general education is sharply separated from experience, in which general education precedes specialized, and in which both are firmly separated from paid employment.

The close interaction with the service agency transforms the agency into a supplementary educational institution. And, through interaction with the college, the agency reexamines its organization of work and staffing patterns. We believe that many of our existing institutions with professional and paraprofessional programs will and should incorporate this approach in some of their curricula. Whether or not they do, we believe that there is also considerable merit in experimentation with these approaches by new institutions fully committed to the combined learning-service principle.

The ideas that underlie these experimental approaches to higher education are, we believe, of particular value in an urban setting. As in any experiment, great care must be taken that the ideas are served well in their applications. Rigorous and continuous assessment of the quality is essential now more than ever in both traditional and experimental approaches to higher education. Persons responsible for experimental programs, in particular, need to be careful to assure that the development of the experiment will give it a fair chance as a successful model for others to follow.

As is evident from Appendix C, the pattern of higher education resources varies from city to city. In some cities, the most urgent need might be for establishment of a new community college or four-year comprehensive college, particularly if the present institutional base is severely deficient. In addition to an adequate traditional institutional base, however, we believe that many metropolitan areas may benefit from modification of programs at existing institutions or establishment of new institutions which are designed to utilize available educational resources in the urban area and to meet urban area and to meet urban student needs.

We recommend that both planning agencies and urban-located institutions review and analyze the educational resources in their areas and the educational needs of urban students to determine whether use of such experimental approaches as those described above, or others that may be developed are desirable to expand effective options for postsecondary educational opportunities in the metropolitan areas.

11. Urban Studies

One of the major educational responses of a university or college to the problems of the metropolitan area is the inclusion within its curriculum of courses designed to teach students about such problems and to train the technicians, professionals, and leaders who will work toward the solution of these problems. Recent years have seen the development within many universities of a variety of courses and programs designed for this purpose. Perhaps the earliest of these courses were concentrated in environmental design departments and took the form of urban planning and design courses and programs.

As more understanding was gained of the nature of urban problems, it became clear that programs must cross the traditional academic discipline lines utilizing a multidisciplinary approach. This led to the development of multidisciplinary seminars, group majors, and eventually to the establishment of multidisciplinary departments focusing on urban studies.

Both undergraduate concentrations in urban affairs, and specialized masters courses are now available at many institutions. In a study of 400 urban institutions, 100 responded that they had either minors or majors in urban affairs or some aspect of it. A recent directory of undergraduate urban studies programs lists 75 such programs and notes that approximately 60 have been in existence less than four years (Bischoff, 1972). Henry Bischoff identifies the main characteristics of these programs:

The main emphasis is on understanding the complexities of urban reality particularly through the social sciences and increasingly in interdisciplinary ways; there is a rather widespread concern for social change and action; there is much interest in goals, norms, and values; there is considerable experimenting with different methods of teaching and learning, especially through action and research involvement in the community; and there is much student participation in the policy formation of the programs. There is growing interest in the problematic question of whether or not urban studies can develop a methodology of its own. Some efforts are being made through such approaches as community analysis (ibid, p. 8).

Some institutions have gone beyond the development of degree programs and have established schools with an urban orientation. The College of Urban Sciences was established at the Chicago Circle Campus of the University of Illinois in 1970 to provide a multidisciplinary focus for professional education and applied research toward the major problems of modern urban society. It is anticipated that the College of Urban Sciences will organize its faculty and students in terms of "task forces" or similar functional groups concerned with major types of urban problems. Initially, a master's degree in urban policy or in various specialized aspects of urban professional activity will be offered. Later, undergraduate degrees will also be offered. The work for all degrees in the College of Urban Sciences will be closely related to the research and public-service programs of the college. Undergraduates would take courses in the social and behavioral sciences, and in other related fields, for a substantial portion of their curriculum during the first two years. During their junior and senior years they would concentrate on the study of urban problems, which would include special courses and seminars, participation in community projects, and involvement in the research activities of one or more task forces.

It should be noted that major universities, wherever they are located, may develop effective urban studies programs within their curricular offerings. It is the urban-located institution, however, that has an excellent and immediate laboratory for its faculty and students.

It is not always necessary to add new colleges or even degree programs to make the curriculum of an institution more responsive to the problems of the city. In the Carnegie Commission survey of student attitudes, 91 percent of the undergraduates at all institutions believed that the curriculum should be more relevant to contemporary life and problems. And certainly among today's problems in society, the problems of the city weigh heavily. It is very doubtful that all of these students were interested in majors in urban affairs, but it is likely that many of them felt that many faculty members, whatever their field of teaching, should make greater efforts to relate their subject matter to today's culture—largely an urban culture. It is characteristic of today's institutions of higher education that efforts to develop an urban emphasis in the educational programs resulted in a few specialized programs rather than a pervasive point of departure in many programs. The latter is certainly more difficult to obtain and requires the active participation of a much larger proportion of any given faculty.

Elden Jacobson lists the reasons why he feels many urban studies programs fall short of the mark for which they were established:

(a) Colleges, virtually without exception, have organized knowledge into a series of conceptual categories called disciplines.

(b) Learning is imagined to consist in transmitting the information each discipline contains.

(c) The structure of the city, however, is increasingly recognized as demanding conceptual categories that transcend, and are significantly different from, the traditional disciplines.

(d) Learning, especially within the urban context, involves information, to be sure, but additionally demands elements of experience, the capacity to empathize, value judgments about justice and the future organization of the social order, that have at no time in recent academic history resided easily within the college's self-understanding.

Jacobson concludes that study of urban matters relates to concepts of "wholeness, humanness, and purpose. And the college, save in its occasional ceremonial rhetoric, lays no visible claims to them" (Jacobson, 1972, p. 295ff.).

The problem described by Jacobson is the problem of making liberal education relevant to today's society, whether that society is urban or nonurban. While higher education has been somewhat successful in training specialists who have expertise in certain matters essential to the governance and development of a metropolitan region, successes with vital multidisciplinary studies are much less common.

To cope with the problems of the cities, Andrew Greely (1970, pp. 232–235) believes the graduates of the 70s should have 12 characteristics and urges that these characteristics be accepted as goals for urban studies programs.[1]

---

[1] Greeley (1970, pp. 232–235) believes that the graduates of the seventies:

1. must be capable of understanding the problems and their complexity and resist meeting such problems with simplistic slogans . . .

(Footnote 1 continued)

2. must be more than intellectually competent; he must be open to his own emotions and those of others . . .

3. must have compassion for other human beings, whoever and whatever they may be . . .

4. must be capable of realistic responses to human problems instead of romantic perfectionism that demands . . . that society reform itself on the morrow . . .

5. should be convinced of the need for competency in solving problems and coping with issues . . .

6. must be capable of long-run commitment to the solution of social problems . . .

7. must be able to see the big picture instead of focussing on one segment, much less glorifying in the narrowness of his focus . . .

8. should be able to organize resources and articulate arguments to develop a climate for public consensus for the solution of urban problems . . .

9. should be sensitive to suffering, wherever it is, even next door . . .

10. should rejoice in diversity rather than be threatened by it . . .

11. should be capable, learning from the wisdom and experience of the past rather than narcissistically believing it necessary to start with a clean slate . . .

12. should seek clinical, objective, and pragmatic solutions without the need to project his conflict with his parents into fantasies of collective guilt . . .

12. Research on Urban Problems

Universities have traditionally considered research activities as their major contribution toward the development of solutions to urban problems. In many cases, the initial response of a university to community demands was the establishment of a research center concerned either largely or exclusively with urban problems. There are now some 300 of these centers linked to various colleges and universities. The centers vary considerably in their organizational structure, their activities, and their patterns of interaction with policy makers in urban areas. There are, however, two elements that are central in most of the structures that have been created by universities:

- Generally the effort is multidisciplinary.
- In most instances attempts have been made to achieve interaction between the research activities and policy makers in urban areas.

In many of these centers, there seems to be greater emphasis on applied or service research than on more basic research and, in many instances, research aspects are closely mingled with action aspects of a project.

While the establishment of urban centers seemed a natural response to universities, communities did not always view them as an appropriate response. A recent report on a study of community involvement of universities summarizes the reaction to urban study centers of various constituency groups:

. . . urban centers have not met any real needs and in some cases have exacerbated tensions between community and university by appearing to be a child of the university's bad faith. They are perceived as collecting data which they use for their own rather than the city's or community's

65

purposes, as being university-sheltered consulting firms, as being expensive and useless, as imposing themselves instead of coming only when asked — as being, in short, empty and foolish gestures. The demand for problem-solving and technical assistance is for something different from what universities are now doing (Organization for Social and Technical Innovation, 1970, p. 20).

Thus some centers fell short as problem-solving and technical-assistance agencies, partly because their mode of operation was more like that of a research agency of the university; on the other hand, research activities of the centers were viewed by many within the university as either parochial research or simple data collection.

In the Center for Planning and Development Research at the University of California, Berkeley, efforts have been made to develop a mode of interaction between the university and the city which will satisfy the educational needs of those involved as well as providing research support for the city. Under this approach, graduate students are loaned to the city of Oakland to be of general assistance and to conduct studies leading to policy recommendations. A significant feature of the project strategy is that graduate students perform research related to policy questions and, since each student works approximately half-time with the policy makers responsible for their particular issues being researched, the policy and action concerns are constantly interwoven. All the doctoral students in the project attend a seminar in the application of social science theory to public policy. Among recent projects undertaken were a financial capability study of Oakland's revenue resources, an evaluation of alternative revenue sources, and an inventory and analysis of the $100 million worth of federal programs used by Oakland.

URBAN OB-SERVATORIES Another vehicle which has attempted to provide urban-oriented research is the network of Urban Observatories. In 1967, Mayor Maier, then cochairman with Robert Wood of a National League of Cities Standing Committee on Urban Observatories questioned:

Even in a presumably scientific age, how often are our municipal decisions guided by the folklore of urban navigation? . . . all too often, I believe, our cities are governed by rule of thumb rather than by the rule of science.

Maier noted Kenneth Boulding's notion that sample surveys are "the telescope of the social sciences" which permits the observer to scan the social universe. Maier felt that a great expansion of the social information collecting system was possible which would replace the folk knowledge of cities with scientific knowledge (Maier, 1966, p. 1). By 1968, six observatories had been established, and this number was expanded to ten in 1969.[1] Each of the observatories was federally funded through the Housing and Urban Development Department at an average of $75,000 annually.

The objectives of the Urban Observatories are:

1 To facilitate making available to local governments university resources useful for understanding and solving particular urban and metropolitan problems.

2 To advance a coordinated program of continuing urban research, grounded in practical experience and application, relevant to urban management, human resources, and urban environmental and developmental problems.

3 To advance university capabilities to relate research and training activities more effectively to urban concerns and the conditions of urban living.

The urban-observatory program, as structured and operated, is basically a city program. The research undertaken, although approved and funded by HUD, is to be the research perceived to be needed by mayors and other city officials, in consultation with university representatives. Each Urban Observatory carries out two types of research activities—network or national research projects and local projects. National programs are undertaken by all observatories on a coordinated comparable basis. The purpose of these projects is to increase significantly the body of generalizable data that may be applicable to all cities and to produce findings and conclusions that will be transferable to other cities throughout the nation. Local research projects are those of particular interest to the individual city.

Each of the ten cities organized its own observatory, and there is substantial variation in the organizational form selected. In four cities a local university functions as the observatory, in one city a university foundation is the observatory, in three cities a nonprofit corporation has been created under state law to act as the urban observatory, in one city a city agency was created, and in one city the state legislature authorized creation of a legal corporation. Regardless of the form, each of the observatories is governed by a

---

[1] The ten cities are Albuquerque, Atlanta, Baltimore, Boston, Cleveland, Denver, Kansas City, Milwaukee, Nashville, and San Diego.

board which includes city and university representatives and in some instances representatives from school districts, county governments, metropolitan and regional planning agencies, suburban jurisdictions, and state agencies.

The observatories have experienced some problems which, in most instances, were inherent in the city government and academic community and in the differing perspectives of the participants in these two environments. Academics and city officials operate in different time frames; and while the mayor is looking for a practical, policy-oriented report, the academic person may be more interested in the theoretical aspects of the problems presented to him. Problems also arose concerning the degree of independence of the university researcher, particularly with reference to the national research projects, and also over the timing of the release of reports. Notwithstanding these problems, a number of projects have been completed which have supplied useful information, and evaluation of the first three years of activity provides support for the continuation of the observatories.

Research on urban matters is complicated by the fact that no satisfactory methodology for basic social science research, parallel to that for physical or biological science research, has yet been devised. As a result, much of the social science research falls in the uncomfortable category of neither qualifying as basic research nor being sufficiently practical to qualify as good applied research. Good applied research is undoubtedly facilitated by an organization such as the urban observatories in which the research client is a prime mover in defining the research need.

13. Public Service

The American university is usually described as having three major and complementary functions—teaching, research, and public service. These three are often spoken of as equally important with each essential to the strength of the other two. Yet the distinction among our institutional types (i.e., lack of emphasis on research in a college) and determinations of levels of quality are almost always made today on the basis of teaching and research without reference to the scope and quality of the institution's public service programs. In the last half of the nineteenth century after the passage of the Land-Grant College Act, effective service to agriculture undoubtedly constituted one of the measures of great land-grant institutions. But, as land-grant institutions emulated other major research universities and as concern with agriculture became a proportionally smaller part of the total institutional endeavor, the importance of public service as a determinant of quality diminished. This may result in part from the fact that the service which the nation seemed to demand of its universities in the middle of the twentieth century was scientific research. While all of society was affected by this scientific activity, relatively limited elements of society interacted with the university in relation to it. Service to agriculture, on the other hand, had resulted in a much broader interaction between higher education and rural America, which was at that time a large element in American society. Thus the expression of the public service function through scientific research and consultation has been viewed primarily as research rather than as public service. Today there are demands that higher education do for our cities what our colleges and universities have done in the past for agriculture. This may lead to a renewed emphasis on this component of the modern university. Exactly how this emphasis is to be expressed and by which institutions is yet to be decided. Providing public service to the cities promises to be a more intricate and perplexing task than providing service to agriculture in the nineteenth and early twentieth century.

In the 1860s, higher education resources were severely limited. In this context it was possible to establish many new institutions directly charged with the responsibility of providing service to agriculture. In some cases it was also possible with what constituted substantial federal grants at the time to impress the land-grant function upon existing institutions. But for the most part, existing institutions were not called upon to modify their admissions policies or to adapt their curricula or service functions to meet the changing needs of society. Thus, the desired emphasis in response to the nation's needs could be obtained by making substantial additions to the total resources of higher education. Today, both because the pool of our resources is relatively closer to our needs and because of severe fiscal limitations, it seems likely that this modification in educational mission would have to be accomplished more through substitution and change than primarily through addition.

Furthermore, the problems to be solved in the cities are more difficult to define, require greater use of interdisciplinary approaches, and involve a much more diverse and amorphous set of constituents.

There were also certain prior successes at the time of the land-grant movement that made it possible for substantial and relatively rapid progress. One, there was a stock of knowledge to be exploited; we presently have little in the way of a comparable stock of knowledge about urban problems. Two, there was a general consensus about the importance of the problem at the time of the land-grant movement, and this general consensus carried with it adequate funding. Three, the objectives to be achieved, improvement in the productivity of our agricultural endeavors, were generally agreed upon. Clearly, these conditions are not present today with reference to urban problems.

These factors will make the task more difficult and may add to institutions' reluctance to accept responsibility for public services in metropolitan areas. We believe, however, that higher education must respond to the problems of the city not only through its formal educational programs and research activities but also through renewed emphasis on public service. This does not mean that all institutions must respond to all demands for services. Nor is it necessary that many of the expressed needs of the city be met by institutional action rather than by action of individuals (students or faculty) within the institution.

STUDENT
SERVICES
TO THE
COMMUNITY

In the 31 metropolitan areas with population in excess of one million, the combined student enrollment in institutions of higher education is almost 2.9 million. This concentrated pool of young people, including many who are deeply concerned about the problems of society, constitutes a valuable source of manpower to meet certain of the city's needs. In a recent survey of 400 four-year colleges and universities in urban areas, 92 percent of the institutions indicated that undergraduate students at their institutions were involved in tutoring programs in the community.[1] The tutoring programs usually involve disadvantaged and minority elementary and secondary students.

Student service activities take many forms. Agriculture students from Michigan State University work together with inner-city people in developing community garden cooperatives. The Memphis Area Project South sponsored "clothes closets" for needy families. Many of the tutoring programs, and other types of student service activities, have been initiated by students, are operated by students, and may require little in the way of outside financing.

At several universities, long-established student organizations have served as a primary focus for student service activities. Stiles Hall at the University of California, Berkeley, has performed this function. And Phillips Brooks House at Harvard has traditionally been a center of student service to the community. Currently it is engaged in a number of projects involving tutoring and guidance of inner-city youth, and work in the Columbia Point Housing Project, in mental hospitals, and in prisons. Many of these projects are funded by private or federal grants.

A six month conference on service-learning programs in Atlanta explored the nature of student service programs, considered which programs effectively combined service and learning components, and suggested ways to increase participation in such programs (Atlanta Service-Learning Conference Report, 1970). From their student survey it was clear that students were more concerned with moderate compensation for community services than whether college credit was given. Part-time employment was necessary

[1] See Appendix F.

to meet college expenses for many of the students, but they would far prefer to earn this money in service activities.

The Urban Corps provides a vehicle for students to obtain experience working in local government and at the same time receive pay for it. Eighty percent of the funding for Urban Corps programs comes from the federal work-study program and twenty percent is supplied by the agency for which the student is working. Fifty-seven cities have Urban Corps programs (Management Information Service, 1972).

We believe that the Urban Corps provides an excellent mechanism for giving opportunities to students to have experience in city government and recommend that cities that do not now have such programs seriously consider developing them.

Advanced students in professional schools have, in many cities, established programs in which members of the community can seek their expert advice. The Community Legal Assistance Office at Harvard is an excellent example of such a project. Established by Harvard Law School in 1966, the office provides free services to those who cannot afford to pay for such services. Working under six staff attorneys, more than 100 law students aid low-income residents of Boston with their legal problems. Similar community legal assistance offices are manned by students at many other law schools.

A more integral part of the institution's educational program, but still involving student services to the community, is the practice of using interns in various types of agencies and professions. Thus students in counseling and guidance, social welfare, and public health may serve intern periods in the city schools, and health and welfare agencies. These professional intern programs frequently underplay the service aspects. In fact, in many of these situations, the school or agency is treated more as a laboratory in which the intern can practice under supervision the types of things he will be doing when he qualifies for his license. The service aspect is considered of such negligible value that in many instances the university or college supplying the student is expected to pay the school or agency in which the student acts as an intern.

The ideal student service activity would seem to be a service which was also treated as a learning experience by the university or college. While the student is supplying needed services in the community, the community serves students as a learning resource. Thus the service activity becomes a part of the institution's educational program.

SERVICE BY FACULTY MEMBERS
As individual members of the community, faculty members serve in a variety of citizen capacities, on boards, committees, and as volunteer workers on various projects. While these faculty members often bring to their citizen-tasks their special expertise (e.g., industrial relations professors serving on personnel boards, architects and planners serving on planning agencies, social welfare professors serving on welfare boards), these services cannot be distinguished from those of any citizen performing his civic duty. Faculty members also undertake various types of consulting activities with various city agencies. Unless there is some institutional involvement in such services (e.g., released time), it is difficult to view these as public services of the institution. On the other hand, the faculty member brings to his consulting the knowledge which in part was developed through university-based research. But he contracts for the consulting and receives pay as an individual. Thus the image created is not the service image of the university or the extension-based agricultural consultant whose time and advice appear to be free, but rather the business image created by a cash transaction. The image may be further confused by the fact that the university-based consultant is already receiving full-time pay from the university.

Suggestions to provide services to the city by stimulating activities of individual faculty members through increased rewards to faculty have never adequately addressed some of the factors discussed above. If community service is to be rewarded by the promotion criteria of the university, must it be free to the community? Many faculty members have given generously of their time to aid in solving community problems. If the university considers this a regular part of a faculty member's responsibility, should a minimum of community service time be required before the faculty member has a right to charge for consulting services? Questions such as these will be sharpened as the faculty work-load question is subjected to increased public scrutiny.

INSTITUTIONAL SERVICES
Urban institutions have responded in a variety of ways to community demands for increased services. Some of these responses have been based in urban studies centers. For example, in two such

centers, urban residents have received technical assistance in the preparation of model cities applications, have collected data pertinent to pending policy decisions, and have prepared metropolitan resource indices. Schools of education have undertaken programs to improve urban public schools. Preliminary results of the Commission's inventory on public services indicate that almost half of our colleges and universities are engaged in some form of assistance programs or consultation with public schools. And, as mentioned previously, some law schools, largely through their students, provide legal services to the urban poor. Perhaps the most extensive and expensive institutional service provided is medical care to many metropolitan residents.

Universities and colleges have also sought to serve the community through establishment of store-front educational centers designed to take the university's knowledge and expertise into the inner city. Some institutions have trained students to provide semi-professional assistance to various city groups. The Peralta Community College System in Oakland, California, has established community Development Centers to provide a tangible presence in the community and to disseminate information about the college and about other public services available to residents. Management of each of the centers is put into the hands of community advisory boards, and programs are developed by the boards through questionnaires and canvassing techniques. Programs offered at the centers include short courses, cultural events, regular college courses, and meeting places for community groups.

The several researchers who have studied the centers, although they have pointed out certain problems, have considered them successful outreach efforts. On the basis of his analysis of the centers, Palola and Oswald (1972) concluded that the following factors are essential for success of outreach programs:

- Community involvement in the design and development of the programs
- Recognition of the need to reassess (and modify) accepted certification policies and personnel practices in the selection of Center staff and to seek acceptance of this "new breed" of professional by the regular faculty
- Development of a flexible intra-district structure as well as adequate funding and freedom from the usual formula budgets

Differentiation of educational missions among institutional types would suggest that certain categories of urban service would be more appropriate for some types of institutions than for others. But no such pattern emerges from a review of which institutions have undertaken which services. The decision to provide a particular service seems to be much less a deliberate decision that the service is consistent with both the goals and resources in the institution than it is a result of the interests of some within the institution or a reaction to specific pressures and demands on the institution.

In some of these services the role of the college or university, whatever it may have been initially, has eventually become administrative rather than substantive. That is, the seekers of the service may look to the college or university primarily for financial support for the program, for physical facilities, or for an organizational structure within which the program may operate or within which it may receive private foundation or government grants. It is particularly this type of involvement in service activities that appears to justify the position of those within the academic community who urge the university to leave public service to others and to confine its own activities to teaching and research. But it is possible for an institution to undertake service activities that enhance its educational programs. The service-learning program mentioned above is this type of mutually beneficial service. In a survey directed to the mayors in 31 major metropolitan areas, the mayors' offices saw specially developed educational programs for city government staff members as one of the most valuable public services provided by the university.[2] Although community representatives in a recent study of the demands of urban constituencies asked that some university funds be spent on community problem solving and called for a halt in university expansion into the neighborhood, the most frequently reiterated community demands related to the educational functions of the university. Taken together the demands were a call for the university to change its admissions policies, to develop relevancy in its programs, to extend its educational services to the general community, not just to the young, and to prepare better those who would be working in the community. More specifically, the community representatives said that the university should:

- Encourage large community inputs into training for community service
- Make this training, in part, accountable to the community
- Emphasize contact with the real world far more in training for urban roles

[2] See Appendix G.

- Blend the professor and the community, decentralizing the training process and encouraging community people, not academics, to organize the field experience (Organization for Social and Technical Innovation, 1970, p. 11)

The university is being asked to use its educational expertise to reassess the validity of its own educational programs, and to develop modifications in approaches and programs to improve their effectiveness.

This suggests that the most valuable services that an educational institution could render to its community are centered in the institution's own educational functions.

Universities are not well equipped in many instances to respond directly to requests for certain services from community agencies. Robert Wood attributes the difficulty to the "unnatural basis of their alliance." He maintains that:

. . . user agencies are more organized, emphasize a somewhat rigid hierarchy of personnel, and are preoccupied with the applicability of immediate solutions to agency problem areas. On the other hand, universities are typically rather disorganized, have a history of institutional isolation from the problems of society, require a relatively long period of lead time in taking action, and focus primarily upon the development rather than the application of knowledge. In addition, the tendency to filter their perceptions through traditional university disciplines has on occasion severely compromised the effectiveness of university personnel in examining user agency problems which have a multi-disciplinary basis (Wood, 1972).

While he is describing the formal governmental user agency, with a few variations his analysis would also apply to less formal community groups. This lack of effective rapport, while perhaps more pronounced with reference to urban problems, is not unique to them. It is doubtful that land-grant colleges would have been as useful to the residents of rural America without the intermediate agency—the network of agricultural extension service units. For community services, the independent agency could also permit university personnel to be involved in controversial matters without directly involving the university as an institution. A further advantage of a satellite service agency, or a quasi-university agency, is that it would facilitate drawing on the resources of several institutions within the area. It could act as the service arm of a group of universities and colleges in the area. As a semi-independent service agency, it would also establish a more clearly delineated basis for funding service programs. User groups would, in effect, contract for services through the agency. University services which constituted an essential element of the educational program, such as professional intern programs or medical education would continue to be administered in the university.

We recommend that institutions of higher education undertake those community service activities which:

- Revitalize its educational functions and constitute an integral part of its educational program
- Are within the institutional capacity both in terms of personnel and resources
- Are not duplicative of the services of other urban institutions

We further recommend that quasi-university agencies be established through which faculty members and/or students could provide services, even on controversial matters, without directly involving the university or college in its corporate capacity.

These quasi-university agencies would be separate from the university or college but would draw on its personnel and would act as a broker in the sense of bringing together those who could supply the service with those who need the service.

14. *Impacts on the Life of the City*

The university located in an urban setting is not only an educational institution that happens to be in a city—it is a physical entity and a corporate force that has diverse and major impacts on the life and environment of the city. While we are primarily concerned in this report with these impacts in metropolitan areas, the community impacts of colleges and universities are also of great importance in small- and medium-sized towns. In fact, in instances of large universities in small towns, the impacts of the institutions may be both more readily identifiable and more intense than they would be in a large metropolitan area. It is in the context of the growing urban crisis, however, that these impacts have taken on new significance requiring more conscious efforts on the part of the institution to maximize positive aspects and control potentially negative effects.

These various impacts may best be discussed under four major headings: (1) physical or environmental, (2) economic, (3) social or cultural, and (4) political. Although these categories will be convenient for purposes of discussion, they are somewhat unrealistic. Any given interaction, such as urban-renewal activities of the university, will have economic, cultural, and political overtones as well as a primary environmental impact.

PHYSICAL OR ENVIRONMENTAL IMPACTS C. A. Doxiadis has described the physical impact of a university on a city:

When we first create a campus, it has a normal relationship with the city. Later, the surrounding area begins to decline, and, even later, the completion of the decline is an irreversible trend.

Why does this happen? . . . a specialized area, such as a university, breaks up the normal pattern of communications, both the physical pattern and the social pattern. The boundary areas, therefore, lose in importance and deteriorate. . . . In the normal pattern, streets pass through the campus area. But next, we usually create very strange patterns of isolated buildings, with big areas for parking all around the campus and in its center. In this way, we break the continuity of the urban system, and, as a result, the whole surrounding area deteriorates. Normal patterns are broken down.

. . . Because of the dynamic growth of the university, decline begins in the areas that are in the line of growth. Thus the whole area around the university, including the area where a university may now grow, declines (Doxiadis, 1969).

Although some disagree with Doxiadis' particular analysis, it is clear that some cities have a hostile reaction toward institutions within their boundaries. Indeed the physical presence of the large institutions provides many reasons for potential hostility.

- Uncertain expansion plans of a university can adversely affect maintenance standards of neighboring areas as well as real estate values in such areas.
- Requirement for parking facilities, and the increased traffic burdens in the vicinities of the campus may place an excessive burden on the city.
- Particularly recently, the tendency of "street people and hippies" to congregate around college and university campuses has accentuated further some of the problems created by the physical presence of the campus.
- Student housing patterns, from the viewpoint of some inhabitants of the neighborhood, may have undesirable effects on otherwise attractive residential areas.

It is possible for a campus to contribute in a positive way to the physical environment of the city. Well-designed campuses may include recreational, cultural, and parklike facilities which would not otherwise be available. Although the primary use of these facilities would be by the students and faculty, there are times on most campuses when they are available to others in the metropolitan area. In a recently completed study of four-year urban-located institutions, almost half of the responding institutions indicated that children from the community use the campus facilities for recreation or entertainment and that community groups or organizations not related to the college use their facilities frequently for their activities. To achieve a mutually beneficial relationship between the campus and its physical environs requires careful consideration by both the campus and the city of the long-range physical plans of the institution. There have been striking examples of failure on the part of both the university and the locality to engage in this type of planning. The recent *Report of the Commission on Isla Vista* (1970) describes repeated opportunities and failures to undertake this type of planning in connection with the growth of the University of California at Santa Barbara, and the difficulties at Columbia grew in part from conflict over physical expansion into the surrounding community (*Crisis at Columbia . . . ,* 1968). In recent years universities and colleges have increasingly taken the initiative to plan for their expansion with due consideration to the impact of that expansion on their environs. In some instances, they have taken some responsibility for the condition of the surrounding neighborhood itself. The geographic dispersion of educational programs throughout the metropolitan area may eliminate the need for some campuses to expand as a block into the surrounding city. Further, it provides a nonthreatening opportunity for educational activities to exist in many areas of the city side by side with other activities.

The environs of universities in many large metropolitan areas underwent a marked change following the Second World War. The middle- and upper-middle-class neighborhoods of several metropolitan university districts were being transformed into slums. This trend intensified as increased crime rates and deterioration of housing quality and urban services caused the former residents to move to the suburbs. As a result, some campuses soon became islands in largely hostile seas. Few among their immediate neighbors were alumni or staff. Many of their neighbors had negative images of the university, and the mechanisms for positive interactions to modify those images did not exist.

Although some universities considered moving their campuses into more congenial surroundings, this was not a feasible alternative for major universities with substantial capital investment. Instead, some of these urban institutions have tried to improve their image in the eyes of their new neighbors through some of the service activities discussed earlier in this report. In addition, some institutions have taken direct action to bring about improvement in their immediate environs, to undertake expansions only after involving those of their neighbors who will be affected by the expansions, and to find more imaginative solutions to expansion problems—the University of Chicago is an outstanding example.

URBAN RENEWAL ACTIVITIES During the late 1940s and the 1950s more than 30 institutions of higher education had become involved in urban-renewal projects affecting their surrounding communities. In addition, a few major universities were assuming major responsibility in the business of city rebuilding.

Kermit C. Parsons and Georgia K. Davis compared the processes, objectives, and results of five urban-renewal activities involving major urban universities: Columbia University on Morningside Heights in New York City; The University of Chicago in Hyde Park–Kenwood/Woodlawn District, Chicago; Case Western Reserve University in the University Circle–Glenville areas of Cleveland; the University of Pennsylvania in the West Philadelphia district, Philadelphia; and Harvard/Massachusetts Institute of Technology in Cambridge. In all these renewal programs, specialized organizations were created to work on behalf of the university and related institutions (Parsons & Davis, 1971).

The researchers found that successful urban-renewal programs went considerably beyond improved physical structure. Some of the programs sought to improve public schools, to increase availability of community social services, and to aid development of economic growth in the area. Certain of the efforts of urban renewal were hampered, according to the researchers, by inadequate institutional leadership, inconsistent behavior concerning expansion and renewal projects, and by secretive postures about institutional decisions. Effective university participation in renewal programs required clear determinations of institutional objectives as well as substantial and long-range institutional commitments of energy and staff involvement.

The enactment of Section 112 of the National Housing Act of 1959, as amended in 1961, which had been supported by major urban universities and the Association of American Universities, gave great impetus to the participation of institutions of higher education in urban-renewal activities. This section provides that for every dollar spent by an educational institution or its "non-profit agent . . . for acquisition of land, buildings, or structures within, adjacent to or in the immediate vicinity of, an urban-renewal project, for demolition. . . for relocation of occupants and for rehabilitation of buildings," the city may receive $2 to $3 of federal urban-renewal assistance. The land and the buildings acquired must be used for educational purposes. This section led to joint action by urban universities and city governments in renewal efforts. By June 1967, the date of the latest published Department of Housing and Urban Development Survey, 115 projects utilizing Section 112 credits with a total area of 12,000 acres and almost $500 million in federal grants had been approved.

Title VII of the Housing and Urban Development Act of 1970 provides for federal government guarantees of obligations issued by the developer to finance large-scale, long-term comprehensive community development projects. It is quite possible that environs of urban universities may be substantially improved through projects under this section.

Some universities have gone beyond the usual pattern of funding for urban renewal and have themselves become, in a sense, developers, using endowment funds for rehabilitation or construction not only for university housing but also for low- and moderate-income housing for their immediate environs. During a period when many institutions are questioning the wisdom of serving as landlord to students and faculty, we wonder whether it is sound policy to become landlord or developer to those who are not members of the university. It is one thing to act as a major participant, catalyst, or facilitator in the planning and implementation of urban-renewal programs; it is quite another to invest scarce university resources on any large-scale basis as a general developer.

Julian H. Levi, who served so effectively as director of the South East Chicago Commission has observed that:

Universities and colleges are not civic betterment associations. Their missions — teaching, training, research, and the extension of man's knowledge about himself and his universe — should not be diverted into operations in city planning and redevelopment unless these diversions are essential to the fulfillment of primary missions. It is, however, a tragic fact that these efforts are today essential to the ability of the institutions to fulfill their primary responsibility (Levi, 1961, p. 137).

While few would argue with the fundamental accuracy of this statement, its application as a criterion for any particular university involvement can result in a wide range of conclusions. Nonetheless, we believe that it provides the best general statement of both justification for and the desirable extent of a university's involvement in renewal activities.

ALTERNATIVE SOLUTIONS TO EXPANSION PROBLEMS

Sensitivity to scarcity of urban space is leading universities to find more imaginative solutions to expansion problems.

- Employment of air space over city streets or over railroad yards for the development of building sites

- The creation of "floating" space such as that developed by the Stevens

Institute of Technology when they purchased a 15,000 ton passenger-cargo liner, a former troop transport, and moored it at the foot of the campus to provide housing space for 200 students

▪ The development of joint occupancy arrangements

▪ The greater use of underground space (e.g., the underground facilities at Wayne State, Rutgers, and Washington University)

Certain of the new types of institutions described in Section 5 will also reduce the need for expansion of campuses or creation of large new campuses. Both the Open University and the University Without Walls require less concentration of physical facilities than the more traditional college or university.

The Commission believes that universities and colleges do have responsibility for their impacts on their surrounding environs.

We therefore recommend:

1 That universities and colleges develop long-range plans which give adequate attention to the interaction between the campus and the neighborhood in which it is located

2 That, where appropriate, colleges and universities participate actively in urban-renewal activities, but that only in unusual circumstances should this participation extend to investment of scarce institutional resources in housing development for the general community

3 That institutions limit their need for expansion into scarce urban space by better use of existing space

Long-range plans should be developed with active consultation between officials of the university and the city. To the extent possible, persons in the neighboring area should be kept informed of developments, and mechanisms should be developed to make possible and to encourage their participation at various stages of the planning process.

ECONOMIC IMPACTS There are many ways in which colleges and universities, particularly large universities, affect the economics of the city.

▪ As a builder

▪ As a major employer

▪ As a purchaser of substantial quantities of goods and services

- As a user of city-subsidized services

- As a holder of tax-exempt property

- As a resource that attracts other types of activities and businesses that find it beneficial to be near higher-education institutions

- As a reason for residence in the city of students and faculty who become purchasers and renters of homes and apartments and buyers of goods and services

As employer and purchaser, universities and colleges have not always been aware of their influence upon either the employment patterns of the city or upon the vitality of various city businesses. Personnel policies for nonacademic employees in many major universities have often been far behind the policies of industrial corporations. Often such policy matters were relegated within the college or university structure to a business manager who was several echelons removed from the top leadership of the institution. Personnel policies affecting academic employees were usually the subject of deliberation at high levels, but in the one area in which the university participated in the general labor market of the community—the various skilled and unskilled employees who make up the nonacademic staff—frequently too little attention was paid to any effect the university's policies as employer might have on employment policies in the metropolitan area at large.

The tax-exempt status of college and university property has often been a source of friction between the city and campus. This is particularly true today when city revenue is quite inadequate to meet the growing demands for city funds. Increasingly, colleges and universities, even though tax exempt, are making some payments for services received from the city. The American Council on Education recently reported that one out of three institutions of higher education now pays taxes or makes cash payments "in lieu of" taxes and/or provides direct services in addition to or instead of those provided by local government agencies ("City Taxes and Services," 1971). Of those institutions making such payments, amounts of payments were determined on the following bases (percent indicates percent of institutions for which the basis of determination was used):

38%   Estimated cost of services provided by local government

32%   Fixed proportion of assessed value of tax-exempt property

20%   Fixed contribution based on some arbitrary assumption

15% Locally determined real-estate tax

14% Fixed proportion of revenues from nonacademic, auxiliary enter-
prises

5% Fixed per capita (per student) rate per annum

1% Fixed proportion of total-annual revenues (Caffrey, 1969)

One possible solution that permits expansion by a tax-exempt university and also accommodates to the city's need for maintenance of the tax base has been devised by Yale University. Acquisition by Yale a few years ago of a site for the new Paul Mellon Center for British Art threatened to remove almost a block from the city's rolls of taxable commercial property. Instead Yale has decided to permit stores in the museum's street level and to keep the site on the city's tax roll.

The loss to the city of tax revenue should, however, be put in proper perspective. Caffrey points out that:

In one large city . . . 58 percent of the land is excluded from the tax roster. Of the tax-exempt land, local, state, and federal governments own more than half and use it for such purposes as schools, roads, parks, waterways, offices, and storage areas. Churches are the second largest nontaxpayers. In addition to houses of worship, church-owned properties such as schools, parks, cloisters, residences, libraries, and competitive businesses are not subject to taxes, simply because they are church-owned. Private schools, including colleges, come third. One may question both the volume of the loss occasioned by removing colleges from the tax rolls and the justice of criticizing them and not the government and the churches.

Furthermore, many colleges are actually substantial taxpayers. In Cambridge, Massachusetts, Harvard and M.I.T. come second and third only to the Cambridge Gas and Electric Company as the largest taxpayers; fourth largest is the Boston and Maine Railroad. Princeton University is the largest single taxpayer in its community (Caffrey & Isaacs, 1971, p. 41).

There is no question that the presence within a city of a large university does reduce the city's revenue from taxes. It is frequently argued, however, that this loss in taxes is more than offset by the university's positive impacts on the economy of the city. The question is a difficult one to answer in objective terms, but recently several interesting attempts have been made. The University of Indiana, in studying economic impact, treated foreign students as an export industry and concluded that the 3,453 foreign students attending universities and colleges in Indiana spending about $17.6

million made higher education the fourteenth largest exporter in the state. Researchers at the University of Oklahoma balanced the costs of instruction for out-of-state students against the tuition collected, expenditures, and revenues directly and indirectly attributed to those expenditures and concluded that attraction of out-of-state students resulted in creation of new jobs at substantially little cost. A University of Washington study concluded that the university's operations resulted in a ratio of business actively generated to tax support of nearly 6 to 1 (Strang, 1971, pp. 5–9).

Some universities have undertaken the task of obtaining the answer by using procedures for estimating the impact of a college or university on the local economy developed by John Caffrey and Herbert Isaacs and published by the American Council on Education in 1971. Such a study was recently conducted at the University of Wisconsin. In examining the property tax issue in that study, Strang concluded that: ". . . it appears that the University community pays more than its share of property taxes relative to the rest of the community" (Strang, 1971, p. 102).

The University of Pittsburgh has also recently completed a study of its economic impact (*The Impact of the University of Pittsburgh . . . ,* 1972). That analysis suggests that the economic benefits generated by the University of Pittsburgh more than offset the hypothetical amount which the city would receive in tax income if some other type of enterprise were located on the campus.

Perhaps more important than providing estimates of total economic impacts on the community is the opportunity that these studies provide for analyzing in some detail those activities which result in drains on the surrounding community and those which make positive contributions.

Unfortunately, an institution may bring net positive economic gains to a community without improving the revenue situation of the city in such a direct way as to offset what the city perceives as losses from tax-exempt property. Economic gains of the community are usually reflected in increased business activity, higher income levels, and increased expenditures. These may lead to increased revenue to the state and the federal government through sales and income taxes, but most cities rely almost exclusively on the property tax as their source of revenue. Removal of property from the city's tax rolls through university expansion can be offset in a direct way only by enhancement of the value of the property remaining on the tax rolls. In some cities, this may provide further justification for active participation by universities and colleges in urban-renewal projects.

We recommend that:

1 Colleges and universities seek to assist the surrounding areas through the operation of their employment and purchasing policies.

2 Regardless of rights given them by charter, colleges and universities should pay the usual taxes on any property held by them for non-educational purposes, and when expanding their campuses, should make every effort to develop the property in such a way as to permit its continuation on the tax rolls.

CULTURAL IMPACTS Chancellor Klotsche of the University of Wisconsin, Milwaukee, has asserted that "The urban university that does not aggressively seek for itself a role in fostering the arts is evading a task that it is peculiarly equipped to perform" (Klotsche, 1966, p. 115). A substantial proportion of America's colleges and universities appear to agree with Chancellor Klotsche. In the preliminary results of a study by Verne A. Stadtman of the Carnegie Commission on public service programs in higher education, 37 percent responded that they considered providing a cultural center for the community a very important role for their institution. Another 36 percent considered it an important role and only 4.5 percent indicated that they considered it unimportant.

We also believe that the performing and fine arts create an excellent focus for mutually satisfactory relationships between universities and their communities. Any neighbor of a college or university has experienced the benefit of a campus performing center suitable for concerts. Iowa City, somewhat isolated from the main tours of musicians and dance groups, is now enjoying frequent performances in its new Performing Arts Center on the University of Iowa campus. The residents of Berkeley reaped rich benefits when construction of an auditorium and a concert hall at the University of California dramatically increased the number of cultural events available locally. Students and community residents mingled as members of audiences for both campus talent and visiting artists.

Cooperative arrangements for use of halls are also possible. In the 1960s, Cornell contracted with the Ithaca Festival Theatre for use of the theatre by the university over a period of 20 years, thus providing support for an existing institution in return for its use.

In Fort Wayne, Purdue and Indiana University rely heavily on the Fort Wayne Art Center for its art program.

Cultural enrichment made possible directly or indirectly by the presence of a college or university is rarely singled out as a major service by higher education to the community. Yet it may be one of the most successful interactions between higher education and the community. Institutions should seek ways best suited to them to improve their cultural contributions to the community.

We recommend that the National Foundation on the Arts and Humanities provide grants for university-based cultural activities available to both the campus and its neighbors and for cooperative endeavors involving higher education and city museums and performing arts centers.

POLITICAL IMPACTS Higher education's political impact on cities, particularly small- or medium-sized cities with large universities or colleges, is now gaining new importance. Increasing political awareness of students combined with the newly gained right of 18- to 21-year-olds to vote has resulted in new discussions of the political role of students. Recent legal decisions on voter residency requirements have permitted more students to gain rights to vote in their college communities; student impact on city elections is being analyzed; and city governments are considering new mechanisms both for involving students in city government and for obtaining reliable indications of student concerns and reactions to municipal government actions.

Just as higher education discovered in its efforts to respond to the community that the community was not a single entity, so too are cities becoming aware that student bodies are not homogeneous groups with single sets of interests and responses.

15. Organization for Urban Affairs within the Institution

The ability of most urban-located universities and colleges to respond to urban needs is severely handicapped by failure to reflect this important function in their organizational structure. Harvard's Committee on the University and the City, noting this lack in Harvard's organization, observed that it repeatedly encountered a fundamental problem in the "absence of some central authority within the university that is fully equipped to respond to demands, anticipate problems, formulate policies, and coordinate university efforts with respect to matters that implicate the community . . . " (*The University and the City,* 1969, p. 19).

Harvard was not alone in this organizational flaw. In the late 1960s, colleges and universities across the nation became aware of the lack of any administrative focus for urban-related activities within their institutions. In response to demands that higher education be more responsive to urban needs, presidents sought inventories of current urban-related activities at their institutions. The preparation of such inventories in many larger institutions was itself a formidable task, involving as it did the necessity of canvassing not only individual departments, schools, colleges, and research units within the institution, but also in most instances requiring canvassing of individual faculty members and nonacademic units. And, in some urban campuses, those charged with the management of real estate investment holdings were not always aware of the negotiations between neighborhood housing groups and the university.

On most campuses neither those within the university nor those within the community had a visible office or unit to which they could turn for information on what could reasonably be expected of the university in terms of urban involvement, or what community groups were active and representative with reference to particular problems, or how to obtain funding for a wide range of urban-related activities.

To fill this need, the Harvard Committee on the University and the City recommended establishment of a new vice-president for external affairs who would be charged with responsibility for the Real Estate Office, the Planning Office, and the Office of Civic and Governmental Affairs and would also provide a clearinghouse for information on university-community activities.

Recognizing a similar need, the University of Pittsburgh established the office of vice-chancellor, program development and public affairs, among whose responsibilities was included the Office of Urban and Community Service.[1] The Office of Urban and Community Services was charged with responsibility for determining how the university could respond to the needs of the urban community—specifically the minority urban community.

Many reasons support the desirability of appointing an officer such as vice-president or vice-chancellor reporting to the president or chancellor and charged with responsibility for coordinating and advising on the institution's urban-related activities.[2]

- Urban-related activities typically emanate from a variety of disciplines thus making it inappropriate to lodge responsibility for such activities in any single school or college except perhaps in those instances where there is an urban science college.

- More important, urban-related activities are likely to cross traditional functional lines involving various combinations of service, research, and instruction, as well as affecting the university in its corporate role and thus involving one or more nonacademic units of the institution.

- Today's high priority for urban concerns makes it desirable to lodge responsibility for this area in an institutional officer close to the chief executive officer.

We recommend that large universities located in urban areas appoint a vice-president or vice-chancellor for urban affairs who

---

[1] See the University of Pittsburgh, *The Response of an Urban University to Change, Vol. II, Reports of the Sub-Committees,* 1971, Attachment A. See also University of Pittsburgh, *Plan for an Office of the Urban and Community Services,* 1969.

[2] See also Appendix F which shows that urban universities are more likely to have a multiactivity urban commitment if they have urban affairs officers.

would be concerned with the university-urban interface in terms of the urban impact of the university's educational, service, research, and corporate functions.

Such an officer would be expected to be a student of the dynamics of the metropolitan area in which the institution is located. He should be able to advise those within the university on both the formal and informal power structures that operate within the metropolis and to translate to those within the area the special expertise and appropriate functions of the university and its personnel with reference to urban concerns. The vice-president for urban affairs would act not only as interpreter, but also as broker, in many cases bringing together appropriate units or individuals within the university with the community groups or agencies seeking university action. If quasi-university groups exist for this purpose, the vice-president for urban affairs would act as university liaison with that agency.

We also recommend that an *urban affairs advisory council* including faculty, administration, and student representatives be appointed to consult with the vice-president or vice-chancellor of urban affairs.

The recommendations just stated would be most appropriate for an urban-based university. While the form might be different, urban-located colleges should also reflect through their organizational structure the importance of their urban-related functions.

The urban activities inventories developed by colleges and universities in the late sixties clearly demonstrated that few institutions have developed overall policies to guide the development of institutional urban-related activities. Activities usually resulted from individual interests within the institution or from response to particular community demands and almost always on an ad-hoc basis without reference to any established institutional guidelines or priorities. We believe that the urban impact of a college or university can be more effective if the institution has an overall policy concerning the nature of urban activities which are consistent with its overall educational mission and if determination to continue or embark upon new urban programs is based upon consistency with such overall guidelines.

We recommend that colleges and universities develop overall policies concerning appropriate urban activities for their institutions to avoid response to new proposals on an ad-hoc basis without reference to consistency with the educational mission of the institution.

16. Toward an Urban Commitment

The relation between campus and city has many facets. Special urban-related activities at many colleges and universities have earned for them some degree of recognition as colleges with an urban mission. Among these are:

- The University of Chicago and the University of Pennsylvania with their early and continued involvement in urban development projects.
- Wayne State, Temple, and City University of New York with their continuing efforts to respond to educational needs of the city.
- Northeastern with its continued growth in the effective use of the cooperative education model, including the recent development of legal education through cooperative education.
- Harvard, Tufts, and Boston University in the development of medical care programs.
- Federal City College with the establishment of an open-admission institution for inner-city residents and the development of related service programs.

This list could be greatly expanded. These are but a few examples of institutions that have developed special urban missions affecting one or more of their institutional functions.

While some have argued that it is almost impossible for a university to be great and also to have a clear urban commitment, there are examples of universities that have gone far to accomplish both. The University of Chicago is a preeminent example of a major university that has throughout its history been concerned both with quality and with the welfare of its surrounding community and service to it. It has demonstrated a concern for the city and for service that warrants calling it an outstanding example of the "city-service model." Its first president, William Rainey Harper, in developing his plan for the University of Chicago, stated that the motto of the true university would be "service for mankind wherever mankind is, whether within scholastic walls or without those walls and in the world at large" (Harper, 1905, pp. 27–28).[1] In keeping with this concept of the university, one of the three major parts of the initial plan for the University of Chicago was a university extension division with its program patterned after British adult extension. The junior college concept was also moved forward greatly by Harper's active support for the notion of a two-year college. And the community college and university extension have been bulwarks of service to the urban community, as we have noted above. Harper also inaugurated the idea of a regular summer school (year-round operations) which created greater opportunities for teachers, junior executives, and others to go to college to improve their knowledge and skill, and at the same time made more effective use of the resources of the university. The divisional organization of the subject matter disciplines (as in the social science division) and the creation of interdisciplinary committees (as the Committee on Human Development) made it more possible to approach problems from the perspective of several disciplines rather than one at a time. And the social sciences have been, during much of the history of the university, outstanding in their quality on a competitive world basis. The interdisciplinary approach and the strength in the social sciences helped lead to unusual faculty interest in urban affairs. Professor Merriam undertook the first great series of studies on the American City; Professor Douglas gave outstanding leadership in municipal affairs; among many other examples. The Industrial Relations Center was one of the first of its kind in the United States and is more oriented toward specific service than almost any other ever has been or is now. President Hutchins gave a seminar in "Great Books" for leading citizens of Chicago. He also was much concerned with improvement of high school education and with articulation of high school and college studies. The Kenwood–Hyde Park–Woodlawn

[1] In the 1920s the University of Chicago undertook a comprehensive local community-research program. The major studies in this program are analyzed in White (1929). Included among these studies were Merriam's *The Government of the Metropolitan Region of Chicago*, Good's *Geographic Background of Chicago*, Jeter's *Trends of Population in the Region of Chicago*, Frixell's *Physiography of the Region of Chicago*, Marshall's and Magee's *Manufacturing Industries in the Chicago Region*, Phillip's *Chicago and the Down-State: A Study of their Conflicts*, and Duddy's *Agriculture in the Chicago Region*.

Community Development and Integration Project under the leadership of the university, begun under President Kimpton, is a great success story. The School of Medicine has provided medical services to local citizens of such importance to them that a high officer of the university has said it could not be withdrawn without the most drastic repercussions. The School of Business has provided unusual opportunities for the intellectual advancement of business executives in the area.

The School of Education has shown great interest in the quality of schooling; and its former dean, Ralph Tyler, is a great authority on and promoter of "assessment" of the results of schooling. The "Chicago School" in economics has furthered greatly the concept of market accountability in the use of resources, and the measurement of the "rate of return" to education as an accountability test. The university has been the preeminent intellectual center for the city of Chicago. The University of Chicago has demonstrated how one of the greatest of universities can also be concerned with its city and with service.

Several institutions are now making new efforts to develop comprehensive urban commitments related to current concerns of urban society—a multifaceted commitment that is expressed through its physical and organizational structure, corporate image, educational programs, research activities, service functions, and through the composition and orientation of its faculty and students.

To help define multidimensional urban roles for itself, the University of Pittsburgh launched a research investigation in April of 1970 funded under a special Office of Education planning grant. The University-Urban Interface Program (UUIP) at Pittsburgh was established "to study, chronicle, and concurrently evaluate Pitt's community relations efforts and innovations, their successes and failures" (University of Pittsburgh, 1972). It was hoped that through this effort they would be able to design ways in which not only their own university-urban relations could be improved but through which they could identify conditions and techniques, and provide insights or guidelines that would aid other institutions in the establishment of improved relations with their communities.

The program at Pittsburgh singled out five subprojects for particular evaluation.

1   Minority and community services, including outreach programs addressed to early detection and prevention of psychological prob-

lems in young children in a predominantly black community; cooperative work with the Neighborhood Centers Association (a community organization funded by the Community Chest) in dealing with neighborhood problems such as housing and racial conflict; a student consultant project which provides free management and consulting services to small business and industrial entrepreneurs in the city's economically depressed black neighborhood; an innovative attempt to introduce theory and practice developed in the university's research laboratories into a ghetto school.

2 A campus development program in which UUIP researchers attempt to identify the consequences of campus expansion and the interaction within and among university, community, and government groups.

3 A communications project in which perceptions of various publics of the University of Pittsburgh will be analyzed in terms of the discrepancies between such perceptions and the realities of the university, with the eventual goal of proposing ways in which various communications channels might be used to provide better communication throughout the university and with its various publics. Included in this communications project are special projects designed to marshall the type of information needed to improve communications such as the study of the impact of the university on the local economy recently completed by the University of Pittsburgh and mentioned earlier in this report.

4 A long-range Pittsburgh goals project which includes a Pittsburgh goals study and sponsorship of a series of forums bringing together community leaders and faculty members to discuss conflict management, the administration of justice, health services, and community goals and the government of the metropolis.

5 University governance for community relations which will utilize data and conclusions generated from the other four projects for the purpose of suggesting the organizational model which would provide the greatest aid for the university in developing its university-community relations.

Whether the University of Pittsburgh University-Urban Interface Program will prove to have the value hoped for it cannot yet be determined. But the project has already generated a number of reports that provide excellent resource material for other universities considering reassessing their own urban commitment.

Another approach toward a comprehensive urban commitment by an institution is that undertaken by Malcolm X College in Chicago. The Palola study provides an excellent historical statement of the college's development as well as a description and evaluation of its present program:

Chicago's West Side is a ghetto community considered by many standards to be the most depressed section of poverty in the city. Basic economic and demographic facts highlight what the living conditions are for the more than 1,000,000 black residents confined to that urban sector. For example, the median family income is approximately $3000 per year, at least 25 percent of the residents are on welfare at any one time, 35 percent of the dwelling units are substandard, with rentals higher for blacks than for whites, infant mortality and tuberculosis rates are among the highest in the metropolitan area, and the incidence of juvenile delinquency is twice that of all Chicago.

Although chronic high unemployment and low educational attainment have long characterized Chicago's West Side neighborhoods, a recent college survey (Morrow & Mapp, 1969) cites Bureau of Labor statistics which show that these conditions have become even greater problems in the past few years. . . .

Recent figures (Weinberg, 1970) show that fewer than 4000 of Chicago's black people attend college on a full-time basis, and that fewer than 10,000 are attending any college at all. Even those who do graduate from high school and are admitted to Chicago's city colleges are ill-prepared for college work. Traditionally, most of them have failed in the community college system (Palola & Oswald, 1972, pp. 79, 80).

It was in this setting that in 1969, a black chief executive was appointed for Crane College, located in the heart of Chicago's West Side. The college proceeded to take several steps to evidence its commitment to urban needs. The name was changed from Crane College to Malcolm X College and the college staff "set upon the purpose of 'total accountability'—an idea which embodies full-scale reciprocity between the West Side institution and the needs of the community it serves. The staff sees the *community,* ultimately, as the college. Thus, the institution is not viewed by the administration and the faculty as simply another inner-city community college with some effective programs for low-income students. Rather, it is being directed toward becoming a totally reconstituted institution organized as a massive community service. As such, the college itself is the program for the disadvantaged" (ibid., p. 84).

Consistent with this approach, the college developed a number of innovative programs and educational alternatives to meet the various needs of West Side residents.

Among these were the following:

1 The *Street Academy Program* directed toward elementary or high school dropouts who are aggressively recruited by the academy and are provided with counseling and guidance to encourage them to enroll in particular training programs. Efforts are also made to provide financial aid for those who do enroll.

2 The *Learning Skills Center,* which operates on a 12-hour daily schedule and provides tutoring services as well as both credit and noncredit courses.

3 The *Learning Resources Center,* a unified new technology facility which provides needed instructional aids for all of the college's programs.

4 The *Community Tutorial Project,* through which college students act as tutors to residents of the community.

5 The *Prison Annex Program,* which provides college preparation for inmates of many of the state's correctional institutions and college work for those who are eligible. The Parolee Assistance Program operates as a part of the Prison Annex Program.

The college is also attempting to develop a working relationship with business, industry, and service agencies in its community both for support of the institution and for eventual placement of the graduates of the institution.

The City University of New York, with its newly established open-admissions program and its long history as a city university, is also moving toward a reassessment of its total urban commitment. Its final expression of urban commitment will undoubtedly differ from that of Malcolm X College since it operates in different communities and has different capabilities as an institution. And, if a major research university undertook a comprehensive urban commitment, it would differ markedly from both of these. But the important observation to be made from the several efforts now underway and from proposals for new efforts is that institutions are exploring exciting new approaches better to serve urban needs. Unfortunately, the institutions seeking to launch the most comprehensive programs are the most seriously handicapped by lack of adequate funding. In a period of financial stringency it is difficult to obtain risk capital from traditional support channels for the purpose of making sweeping changes in educational missions. We be-

lieve that the federal government is, however, in a position to provide this risk capital to carefully selected universities which wish to
undertake a reorganization of their institutional program in terms of
a comprehensive urban commitment.

We recommend that an Urban-Grant program be established which
would provide 10 grants to carefully selected institutions for the
purpose of undertaking a comprehensive urban commitment for
their institution. These grants should not exceed $10 million each
for a ten-year period with reviews every two years.

In addition to submitting a satisfactory proposal, any institution
qualifying for a grant must demonstrate that the proposal emanates
from the institution as a whole rather than from individual units
within it, that the proposal has the active support of the administration and the faculty, and that the local *metropolitan higher education council,* if such a council exists, gives general support to the
proposal.

17. Organization for Postsecondary Education in the City

Metropolitan areas have wide arrays of postsecondary public and private educational institutions, including universities, four-year colleges, two-year colleges, and usually some public vocational schools and many private trade and technical schools. While the student is offered a rich selection of educational opportunities, he rarely has adequate information or guidance to use these wisely to meet his educational goals. The institutions themselves may not know enough about their neighboring institutions to consider ways of cooperating to make their own operations more effective. Indeed, it is characteristic of the state of our knowledge of educational resources generally that, although we are interested in the broad range of postsecondary educational opportunities, this report has focused primarily on colleges and universities—the only postsecondary institutions for which substantial and systematically gathered data are available.

Clearly the student needs expert advice and guidance to utilize effectively the abundant educational resources near him. In addition, special institutional arrangements may be necessary to permit him to combine these resources in ways which would maximize satisfaction of his educational goals.

Some of the new types of institutions described earlier in this report, such as Minnesota Metropolitan State College and Universities Without Walls, do act as educational facilitators for their students. Such institutions are not concerned with directly supplying to the student all the educational services he needs. Instead, working from the student's educational needs and knowledge of resources in the area, they serve as brokers, matching resources and needs.

This general philosophy also underlies planning by the Syracuse University Research Corporation (SURC) in its development of a comprehensive system of extramural, postsecondary educational opportunities for central New York. Initial plans for providing external degree options through this project entail counseling the candidate in the best use of the varied educational resources in the five-county region and in developing cooperative arrangements among the institutions to facilitate their use by external degree candidates.

In keeping with this philosophy, one of the first activities of the project was to survey learning facility resources within the five counties. Figure 1 shows the availability within the area of public high schools, colleges and universities, public libraries, museums, businesses with "in-house" programs, and churches.

Project staff members concluded that "in spite of a chronic shortage of adequate shelter for housing in the United States, shelter for purposes of learning and schooling is in super-abundance. . . . within a few minutes drive of anyone's home in the five-county area are school and university facilities, commercial and industrial facilities, religious and civic facilities, or museum and library facilities, that are used for their prime purposes only a limited number of hours a week. The rest of the time many of these facilities remain unutilized. Each one of the under-utilized facilities becomes a potential study center, learning center, guidance center, or small-group meeting center for those preparing themselves for an external degree" (*XD Newsletter,* 1971).

Tentative plans for the project call for a secretariat of the external degree consortium which would provide guidance and counseling services to help the external degree candidate match his educational needs with available resources.

Thus certain experimental institutions are beginning to provide postsecondary educational counseling services. But as yet these services are available to only a very small proportion of the many who would benefit from them.

To many of its residents, the metropolitan area constitutes a natural educational market. But metropolitan areas have not generally been viewed as the appropriate unit for developing and coordinating educational resources. Only a few of the 31 metropolitan areas with populations in excess of 1 million have functioning coordinating agencies; none have a postsecondary educational counseling agency available to all in the community and providing advice about all educational resources within the community; and few of the central city governments within major metropolitan areas include anyone on the staff with special responsibility for liaison with higher education, or more broadly, with postsecondary education.[1] Control, co-

[1] See Appendix G.

FIGURE 1 *Central New York preliminary review learning facility resources*

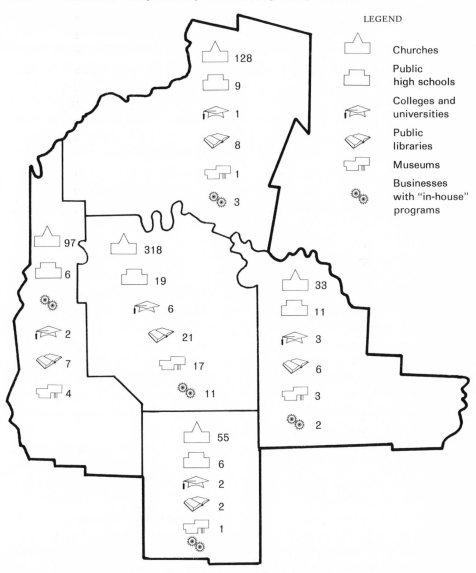

NOTE: All numbers tentative pending final survey results.
SOURCE: *XD Newsletter,* 1971, p. 2.

ordination, and planning are usually the function of state agencies, and the state is also the major source of funding for most public colleges and universities, the notable exception being community colleges in certain states.

Nonetheless, institutions existing in the metropolitan region, which compete to some extent for the same students, which deal with some of the same metropolitan agencies, and which relate to the same industrial and social structure of the region, have a different relationship with one another than with other colleges and universities located outside the region. In those metropolitan regions which include more than one state, public institutions may be under the jurisdiction of different state agencies, thus making impossible effective metropolitan coordination through a single state agency.

Recent developments in both the population patterns of metropolitan regions and in higher education enrollment trends make it particularly desirable to achieve coordination among institutions in metropolitan areas.

- While an overall shortage of college spaces continues in many metropolitan areas, excess capacity at higher tuition private institutions is increasing, while public-college enrollment grows.

- Metropolitan institutions, many severely hit by the new depression in higher education, can alleviate in some measure their financial problems by sharing facilities with other colleges and universities.

- In some instances coordinating agencies may seek to obtain agreement on differentiation of functions among institutions within the region to avoid unnecessary duplication and/or to protect particular markets for certain institutions.

- A consortium or metropolitanwide agency may be organized to provide certain educational or service programs beyond the scope of the individual cooperating colleges.

- Growth of population in the central cities has either declined or slowed considerably in the last decade while population continues to grow rapidly in the suburban areas within the metropolitan regions, thus suggesting that the location of today's institutions might not be desirable for population patterns which will exist a decade or so in the future.

- The nature of the central-city population is also changing and the capabilities of some central-city institutions may not fit the particular educational needs of the residents of the area. Cooperation with other institutions in the central city could provide the desirable range of educational services.

These factors have led to the development of various types of consortia or voluntary coordinating agencies in some of the nation's metropolitan areas. The following brief descriptions will provide examples of the types and purposes of such agencies.

In 1965 five private institutions formed the Pittsburgh Council on Higher Education. A sixth college was admitted to the council in

1969. The council is incorporated as a nonprofit corporation and operates primarily as a consortium of the six institutions. Its board of trustees consists of the president or chancellor plus two trustees of each of the institutions. It was not until 1971 that the council established a central office. The council's development was aided by foundation funding. Recent activities include cross-registration programs at member institutions, thus providing an expanded range of educational offerings to individual students—development of plans to improve interlibrary loans with privileges to students at member institutions, development of a *Pittsburgh Education View Book,* review of black-studies programs at member institutions, and preliminary planning for a joint modern-languages program.

The Cleveland Commission on Higher Education, established by five private institutions in 1956, now includes all the eight public and private institutions in the greater Cleveland area. The commission operates as a general-purpose consortium but also has conducted the type of needs studies more typically undertaken by coordinating agencies. For example, in 1959 the commission issued a study demonstrating the need for establishment of a community college in the Cleveland area and launched a three-year campaign to obtain support for establishment of such a college. In 1964 Cuyahoga Community College was established. Other activities of the commission have included origination of a joint collection system for NDEA loans; a joint project with the public schools in the area to improve student teaching; and a project (HELP) to develop a communitywide, comprehensive program to assist inner-city high school graduates in the Cleveland area to continue their educational careers at nearby colleges and universities. The commission has also provided a number of informational programs for member institutions and informational publications for Cleveland students. The Cleveland Commission on Higher Education is supported in part by assessments on member institutions but also receives corporate and foundation support.

In 1972 a Regents Advisory Council was established for higher education in New York City. The advisory council was asked to develop task-force reports and staff studies concerning public and private higher education in New York City with the goal of presenting a New York City regional plan to the New York State Board of Regents. A basic concept on which the council operates is that all higher education institutions, both public and private, should be considered as a single resource committed to the common goal of providing an opportunity for participation in a program of postsecondary education for every citizen of New York City who wishes it. The strong planning and coordinating thrust in the New York council's purposes distinguish it from the more limited goals of even those metropolitan consortia with relatively broad general purposes.

Originally established by the board of regents as an interim one-year council, the Regents Advisory Council is now recommending that it be continued, that its functions be broadened, and that its scope be expanded to include all postsecondary education including proprietary schools. The board of regents have also established a Northeast Regional Council and a Genesee Valley Council, and plans for establishing others are under way.

In Denver, a somewhat different approach to coordination was undertaken. In 1971, the Auraria Higher Education Center was established to provide a downtown higher education complex, particularly for community students. At that time new metropolitan colleges were to be established, and it was decided that each would be enhanced if they were to be located in close physical proximity to one another. The development of the Auraria Center was made possible, in part, by a federal urban-renewal grant and by state and city funds. Operating in the Center are the Community College of Denver-Auraria, Metropolitan State College, and the University of Colorado, Downtown Center. The Center is governed by a Board of nine members with three appointed by the governor and the president and one trustee from each of the institutions sharing the Auraria site. The Center hopes to develop certain facilities that will be used in common by all institutions in the Center, such as a learning resources center including a library, a heating-cooling plant, creative and performing arts center, and various recreational facilities.

A number of special-purpose consortia exist in many metropolitan areas. One such consortium of special interest in connection with this report is the recently established Consortium for Urban Education in Indianapolis (CUE). The Indianapolis CUE recently presented a workshop for inner-city elementary teachers and professors of education for the purpose of pinpointing current deficiencies in the preparation of inner-city teachers and proposed means to eliminate them. Many metropolitan consortia exist for the purpose of sharing programs, facilities, or personnel. In recent years the development of cross-registration programs has become a very important function of many metropolitan consortia.

While metropolitan consortia yield varied benefits, the potential for effective coordination of educational resources and provision of needed student services is limited. As mentioned earlier, we believe that the higher education needs of the metropolitan area call for modification of some existing institutions, establishment of additional traditional colleges in some areas, and inauguration of new types of higher education institutions designed to better serve the metropolitan area. To ensure better use of both existing and new institutions, and to aid the individual to achieve the best use of available postsecondary educational resources, most major metropolitan areas should establish two new agencies. It is expected that these agencies might vary in exact nature from area to area depending upon the higher education resources in that area, but the central purposes of agencies in all areas would be similar. One of these agencies, the *metropolitan higher education council,* would be primarily a planning and coordinating body working among institutions, between institutions and industry, and between institutions and various types of service agencies. These councils might be formed by modifying and expanding the scope of agencies already in existence (e.g., broad-purpose consortia now in operation). The other agency, the *metropolitan educational opportunity counseling center,* would relate primarily to the educational consumer and attempt to facilitate his educational experience.

METROPOLI-TAN HIGHER EDUCATION COUNCIL

In certain metropolitan areas an already existing consortium, such as those described above, could form the nucleus of the proposed *metropolitan higher education council.* None of the existing organizations, however, has the full range of responsibilities we would suggest for the council. Specifically, the council would:

- Act as primary market-research agency for educational needs in the metropolitan area and as central focus for planning for higher education in that area. The council would work closely with any existing state coordinating agency on assessment of needs and in educational planning. With its primary focus on the metropolitan area, however, it would play a key role in the continuing evaluation and implementation of recommendations for higher education in the area.

- Create a vital, working system of interaction between industry and education in the city. This could be accomplished in a number of ways: (1) working with industry and appropriate colleges and uni-

versities to institute in technical and professional fields a series of
work-study programs in which employees alternate periods of work
with intensive seminars on academic material related to that work;
(2) arranging with colleges and universities a series of late after-
noon classes in factories or office buildings; (3) helping industry assess its educational needs for its various positions and by working
with placement officers to develop new screening techniques with
reduced reliance upon degrees as sole screening devices.

- Develop a cooperative working relationship between appropriate
  metropolitan colleges and universities and the public school system
  to develop projects designed to (1) improve inner-city teaching, (2)
  facilitate early admission and advanced-placement programs
  for high school students, (3) act as a placement agency for student
  teachers in the city schools from all the city's colleges and universities.

- Serve as the coordinating agency for student service projects in the
  community. This agency would perform a function similar to that
  proposed by the Atlanta Service-Learning Conference. It would act
  as receiving agent for work-study funds to be dispersed through
  community agencies and would be responsible for placing students
  with various agencies and providing supervision in the appropriate
  use of these students. While the agency would provide some general
  orientation for students on service projects, it would not provide
  educational programs or grant credit in connection with any service
  activities. The educational content of any program or supervision of
  the student in his service assignment for educational purposes
  would be the function of the college or university at which the student is matriculated.

The council would serve as a lay board representing the educational interests of the metropolitan area. Its members might receive
their positions in a number of ways, but it would probably be most
advisable to have a portion drawn from higher education, and one
or more appointed by the governor and one or more by the appropriate mayor or mayors.

While the Secretariat of the council would be responsible for administration of the council's program, it is assumed that the council
would appoint task forces or contract for any needed research. The
council would, of course, establish the broad policies within which
the secretariat would function.

METROPOL-ITAN EDUCATIONAL OPPORTUNITY COUNSELING CENTER The center would be designed to encourage more effective use of the educational resources in the area by the educational consumer. Counseling burdens of universities and colleges have increased in recent years. At least that portion of the burden not related to the particular institution could be handled at the center, and new demands to universities for expanded counseling could be examined first in terms of whether it would be appropriate to channel the activity through the center rather than adding functions to the university. Specifically the center would:

- Act as educational and vocational adviser to the citizens in the metropolitan area, regardless of their age or past educational preparation. At the present time our staffs of educational and vocational advisers are woefully inadequate, both in numbers and often in training, and may be limited in their approach because of their institutional connections. Where today does the man of 40 who wishes to change vocations, or the woman who wants to return to school after her children are old enough, go for expert free educational counseling? Each could go to a dozen institutions in the area and receive some advice, but understandably, this advice is rarely concerned with the whole range of alternatives open to the individual. Instead, it is limited to those options available to the student through the institution he is consulting. Today's high school student or community-college student is somewhat better served; even for these students, however, a recent poll shows that only a small fraction of teen-agers in the country feel that they have as much information as they need in order to decide intelligently on a future career (Opinion Research Corporation, 1970). Furthermore, the need for expert counseling may be greatest among those who are no longer students—the early high school leaver, or the community-college dropout.

- Act as adviser to the higher education council on the need for new facilities and on any discernable shifts in student educational demands. As use of these centers becomes more prevalent among consumers of educational services, the center will be in a position to provide, both through its daily contact and through systematic studies, educational market information to aid the *metropolitan higher educational council* in planning new educational facilities and programs.

Because the opportunity centers are designed to serve the potential student, their activities should be carried on at a number of locations dispersed throughout the metropolitan area. They would not, however, require the construction of new facilities. The centers could conduct their activities in any available space in public and private colleges and particularly in community colleges, in local public libraries, and in any other space that could be made available on a continuing basis and which would be readily accessible to substantial numbers of potential students. Initial interviews or limited services might also be made available at a variety of places where it might not be desirable or feasible to establish permanent offices of the center—for example, booths in public parks, at public fairs, and at industrial plants or office buildings. Depending upon the geographic characteristics of the metropolitan area, mobile units might also be used to provide limited services.

Broad policies, determination of program priorities and staff leadership for the opportunity centers should be determined by a center governing board, some of whose members might be appointed by the governor and some by the appropriate mayor or mayors. Those with appointment authority should be charged with including in the membership of the board representatives of colleges and universities; public and private trade, vocational, and business schools; public and private high schools; metropolitan and/or city government agencies; and industries and unions operating in the area. In implementing its programs, the board and staff should consult with established neighborhood organizations and, if none exists, should seek other ways to obtain the perspective of residents of various neighborhoods.

While the *metropolitan higher education council* could undoubtedly function quite well with a small professional center staff, the opportunity centers, to be effective, will have much heavier staffing needs. With carefully designed assignment responsibilities, it might be possible to meet some of these staffing needs through use of advanced students who are seeking service opportunities. A continuing training program in educational counseling would provide some staff services from student trainees, and for school and college counseling personnel on rotational training assignments to the center.

The opportunity centers and metropolitan councils are neither designed nor intended to be higher education institutions and they should not be considered a part of city or metropolitan governments.

They are independent civic agencies seeking cooperation among and providing services to colleges and universities in the area and acting as educational facilitators for residents of the area. Moreover, they are not conceived of as creatures of any existing state coordinating or regulatory agency. For liaison purposes, however, a representative of any existing state higher education agency should sit as an ex officio member of the boards of these agencies in his state. And, also for liaison purposes, the executive director of the opportunity center should serve as an ex officio member of the metropolitan council board and the executive director of the council should serve as a member of the center board. Funding for these agencies will be discussed in the next chapter along with funding proposals for other major recommendations made in this report.

In each metropolitan area with population in excess of one million, we recommend establishment of:

1 a *metropolitan higher education council*

2 a *metropolitan educational opportunity counseling center*

We believe that smaller metropolitan areas would also benefit from the establishment of these agencies but consider the highest priority and funding preference should be given initially to the major metropolitan areas.

As noted earlier, few cities have anyone on the city staff with special responsibility for liaison with higher education in the city. We believe, particularly in major cities, that such an assignment of responsibility, which would also include liaison with the proposed *metropolitan higher education council* and *metropolitan educational opportunity counseling center,* would be desirable.

We recommend that mayors of major cities assign someone on their staff primary responsibility for liaison with higher education in the city.

18. Funding for Higher Education in the City

The nineteenth century saw the development of several municipal universities. These were universities supported almost entirely by local taxation and subject to the control of local governing boards. By 1964, only ten of these municipal institutions were still in existence, enrolling 161,456 students. Within the next eight years all but the four colleges of the City University of New York and the University of Cincinnati had been absorbed into state systems, and none of these continued to receive the bulk of its support from the municipality. The City University of New York still receives large subsidies from the City of New York, but at least one-half of its present financing comes from the State of New York. The University of Cincinnati is still municipally sponsored but is now also affiliated with and receives subsidies from the state.

In the twentieth century, the two-year community-college movement developed rapidly. Many of these colleges were initially, and continue to be to some extent, supported by local governments. In many states, state support for community colleges was nominal, but by 1965 two-year colleges were receiving one-third of their support from local governments, one-third from state governments, and the remainder from other sources, primarily student tuition and fees (Medsker and Tillery, 1969, p. 115). The shares varied substantially from state to state (see Appendix H). In 18 states, from 95 to 100 percent of community-college support was supplied by the states in 1967. Over 50 percent of community-college support was supplied by local governments in only seven states in that year.

During the last part of the nineteenth century and the early part of the twentieth century, cities were growing rapidly and consequently their taxable property values increased rapidly also. At the present time, the property base of the cities is not expanding suf-

TABLE 3	Source	Amount*	Percent*
Revenues, 1965–66, public two-year colleges (in thousands)	Local government	$236,773	33
	State government	241,367	34
	Federal government	29,735	4
	Tuition and fees	93,547	13
	Room, board, and all other charges	43,710	6
	Earnings from endowment investments	1,163	1
	Private gifts and grants	2,657	3
	Other sources	46,483	6
	TOTAL	$695,435	100

* Dollar amounts and percentages have been collapsed and rounded.
SOURCE: U.S. Office of Education, National Center for Education Statistics. Adapted from "Financial Statistics of Institutions of Higher Education," *Current Funds and Revenue Expenditures 1965–66,* Washington, D.C. 1969.

ficiently rapidly to meet the growing demands on the cities' revenues. Colleges and universities have increasingly looked elsewhere for financial support.

It is possible that various revenue-sharing techniques proposed by the federal government will improve the revenue situation for the cities, but even with this it seems likely that little of the cities' revenue would be available for funding of their higher-education needs.

In our report, *Quality and Equality,* issued in December 1968 with *Revised Recommendations* issued in June 1970, we recommended that the federal government provide start-up grants for planning and nonconstruction costs for urban institutions, not to exceed $1 million per institution. We reiterate that recommendation and urge that these funds be made available for the types of educational activities and programs described in this report. We also believe that the effective use of existing facilities within metropolitan areas will reduce the need for construction of new facilities.

We further recommend that:

1 Within the level of research funding which we recommended in *Quality and Equality,* high priority be given to both basic and applied social science research

2 The network of urban observatories be continued and that each observatory be funded at approximately $100,000 per year

3 The new National Institute of Education make grants available to those institutions that are conducting systematic experiments with remedial education

4 From funds allocated to the Secretary of Health, Education and Welfare for innovation and reform in higher education, grants be made available for development and testing of new techniques for assessing individual competencies

5 States recognize the public-service demands made on public institutions and provide funds for such services

We also recommended, in *Quality and Equality,* that $30 million be made available from federal funds for counseling programs. Assuming that experimentation in early programs is successful, we would urge that a very substantial part of this funding for counseling be channeled through the proposed *metropolitan educational opportunity counseling centers.*

The opportunity centers will require funding beyond that amount.

We recommend that the centers be funded one-half from local sources and one-half from state and federal sources.

We also recommend that funding for administrative expenses of the metropolitan councils be similarly shared, with one-half from local sources and one-half from state and federal sources.

It is assumed that special projects of these councils would be funded on the basis of public and private grants and contracts.

We recognize that local revenue sources have many competing demands, but we believe that these two agencies can do much to aid residents of the area and to use more effectively educational resources in the area. Effective coordination and counseling might well reduce the demands for extensive local investment in new resources.

There are presently many federal programs that provide funds for a wide range of research, service, and educational activities that might be undertaken by colleges and universities. A guide to federal funding for urban activities was recently issued (American Association of State Colleges and Universities, 1971). This publication lists a wide range of federal programs, provides information on the amount of funding available as well as a description of the programs, and notes contacts to obtain further information. It is unfortunate that federal funding for urban activities presents such a maze to those seeking funds. At the present time, a college or university that wishes to develop an urban orientation with instructional, service, and research components must seek funds from a variety of agencies, under a number of different programs conforming with particular requirements and interests of each program. Both the level of commitment and expertise in coping with bureaucracies must be high to develop the multiagency, multiprogram package that results in funding. A visible focus for urban activities of higher education, such as that available for health and the sciences in the National Institutes of Health and the National Science Foundation, would both encourage and improve the quality of university- and college-based urban activities. We are not recommending the establishment of a new federal institute on urban affairs, although the importance of urban concerns and their complex nature suggests there is some merit to such a proposal.

We do recommend that an Urban-Grants Program be established within the Department of Health, Education and Welfare with a funding of $10 million annually for 10 years.

A portion of these funds could be obtained by transferring to the Urban-Grants Program funds from existing programs concerned with urban activities of higher education. The newly developed Urban-Grants Program would be authorized to make multipurpose urban grants to selected colleges and universities located in metropolitan areas as described earlier.

19. Conclusion

Improving higher education in the nation's urban areas and improving the capabilities of our colleges and universities to serve urban needs are tasks of highest priority. And they are tasks which must be accomplished within a very short time frame. Their accomplishment will require the active cooperation of the many agencies concerned with higher education.

Within higher education we have suggested that:

- Two-year community colleges must undertake major responsibility for increasing initial access to higher education and providing a wide range of vocational and occupational programs.
- Comprehensive colleges are particularly suited to provide many of the services and applied-research needs as well as expanding access to upper-division collegiate work.
- Universities will make their contribution primarily through basic research and professional training.

We have called for the development of additional open-admissions institutions and comprehensive colleges in order to expand access at both the lower- and upper-division levels.

We have urged development of new techniques to utilize excess capacity in existing urban-located institutions. We have also recommended that four-year colleges and universities reexamine their admission policies and practices to provide at least some portion of their admission on a flexible basis.

Throughout the recommendations in this report, we have suggested various responsibilities for particular agencies.

- Within the *urban campus*, we have proposed that the importance of the institution's urban activities and urban relations be reflected in the institution's organizational structure and that the campus develop a policy relating its own educational mission to its urban-related programs.

- Within the *metropolitan area* itself, we have proposed development of two new agencies, the *metropolitan higher education council* and the *metropolitan educational opportunity counseling center.* For both of these agencies, we have proposed that appropriate local governments contribute, along with the state and federal governments, to the support of their administrative expenses as well as sharing authority to appoint members of the governing bodies of these agencies.

- For the *state,* we have reiterated earlier recommendations about the need for continued support for expansion of student places, particularly in community colleges and comprehensive colleges, and have further recommended that states contribute to the support of *metropolitan higher education councils* and *metropolitan educational opportunity counseling centers.*

- We have proposed that the *federal government* have a major responsibility for providing selective national support for several urban programs including partial support for the proposed *metropolitan educational opportunity counseling centers* and *metropolitan higher education councils,* matching funds for construction, continued support of urban observatories, support of research related to urban problems, effective support of innovative programs in higher education designed particularly for the cooperative use of varied educational resources in the cities, support of university- and college-based cultural activities through the Endowment for the Humanities and Arts, and development of a new Urban-Grants Program.

Perhaps more important than any of our specific recommendations is the necessity that colleges and universities, cities, counties, states, and the federal government reassess their activities in terms of positive contributions designed to improve both the quality and quantity of educational resources within our metropolitan areas, and particularly within our inner cities, and effectively to mobilize the research and service capacities within higher education toward the goal of enhancing the quality of urban life. Some of the sense of the immediate crisis in our cities that characterized the late sixties has faded. The present relative calm may falsely reassure us that all is well. The needs are well documented and higher education must find effective ways to make its own particular contributions in response to those needs before waiting for overt crisis manifestations to again develop.

The land-grant college movement was one of the most revolutionary ideas in the history of higher education both in the United States and in the world. It provided the momentum for the development of colleges with a new sense of direction to the needs of a dominant force in American society at that time—rural America. Today we need a similar commitment to direct the attention of our colleges and universities to the concerns of urban America.

Appendix A: Higher Education Enrollment and Population in Metropolitan Areas (1970)

Standard metropolitan statistical area	Higher education enrollment			Population
	Public	Private	Total	
ALABAMA				
Birmingham				
Total	14,251	5,985	20,236	739,000
Central City	11,797	5,253	17,050	297,000
Suburban	2,454	732	3,186	442,000
Mobile				
Total	7,222	1,394	8,616	377,000
Central City	6,136	1,394	7,530	188,000
Suburban	1,086	0	1,086	189,000
ARIZONA				
Phoenix				
Total	58,653	1,860	60,513	968,000
Central City	15,208	1,860	17,068	580,000
Suburban	43,445	0	43,445	388,000
Tucson				
Total	29,613	0	29,613	352,000
Central City	29,613	0	29,613	258,000
Suburban	0	0	0	94,000
ARKANSAS				
Little Rock–North Little Rock				
Total	4,828	1,286	6,114	323,000
Central City	4,828	1,286	6,114	188,000
Suburban	0	0	0	135,000
CALIFORNIA				
Anaheim-Santa Ana-Garden Grove				
Total	67,370	7,128	74,498	1,420,000

Standard metropolitan statistical area	Higher education enrollment			Population
	Public	*Private*	*Total*	
Central City	14,998	0	14,998	441,000
Suburban	52,372	7,128	59,500	979,000
Bakersfield				
Total	11,914	0	11,914	329,000
Central City	11,258	0	11,258	68,000
Suburban	656	0	656	252,000
Fresno				
Total	32,926	520	33,446	413,000
Central City	29,358	520	29,878	162,000
Suburban	3,568	0	3,568	251,000
Los Angeles–Long Beach				
Total	352,341	54,792	407,133	7,032,000
Central City	163,696	42,846	206,542	3,029,000
Suburban	188,645	11,946	200,591	4,003,000
Oxnard-Ventura				
Total	13,940	1,373	15,313	376,000
Central City	8,285	0	8,285	127,000
Suburban	5,655	1,373	7,028	249,000
Sacramento				
Total	64,064	0	64,064	801,000
Central City	46,745	0	46,745	258,000
Suburban	17,319	0	17,319	543,000
San Bernardino–Riverside–Ontario				
Total	48,242	8,792	57,034	1,143,000
Central City	31,820	690	32,510	310,000
Suburban	16,422	8,102	24,524	833,000
San Diego				
Total	87,332	6,274	93,606	1,358,000
Central City	62,688	6,274	68,962	676,000
Suburban	24,644	0	24,644	682,000
San Francisco–Oakland				
Total	175,161	23,140	198,301	3,110,000
Central City	65,713	16,693	82,406	1,063,000
Suburban	109,448	6,447	115,895	2,047,000
San Jose				
Total	70,876	18,606	89,482	1,065,000

Standard metropolitan statistical area	Higher education enrollment			Population
	Public	*Private*	*Total*	*Population*
Central City	47,736	273	48,009	437,000
Suburban	23,140	18,333	41,473	628,000
COLORADO				
Denver				
Total	46,540	12,899	59,439	1,228,000
Central City	19,354	12,899	32,253	513,000
Suburban	27,186	0	27,186	715,000
CONNECTICUT				
Bridgeport				
Total	7,604	15,404	23,008	389,000
Central City	5,415	11,590	17,005	155,000
Suburban	2,189	3,814	6,003	234,000
Hartford				
Total	17,982	13,356	31,338	664,000
Central City	15,300	2,318	17,618	156,000
Suburban	2,682	11,038	13,720	508,000
New Haven				
Total	19,484	18,072	37,556	356,000
Central City	16,474	10,281	26,755	134,000
Suburban	3,010	7,791	10,801	222,000
DELAWARE (N.J./MD.)				
Wilmington				
Total	18,225	2,828	21,053	499,000
Central City	2,071	2,380	4,451	80,000
Suburban	16,154	448	16,602	410,000
DISTRICT OF COLUMBIA (MD./VA.)				
Washington, D.C.				
Total	87,073	67,586	154,659	2,861,000
Central City	10,511	65,932	76,443	746,000
Suburban	76,562	1,654	78,216	2,115,000
FLORIDA				
Fort Lauderdale–Hollywood				
Total	7,077	920	7,997	620,000
Central City	7,077	920	7,997	243,000
Suburban	0	0	0	377,000

Standard metropolitan statistical area	Higher education enrollment			Population
	Public	Private	Total	
Jacksonville				
Total	6,660	5,636	12,296	529,000
Central City	6,660	5,636	12,296	513,000
Suburban	0	0	0	16,000
Miami				
Total	27,950	18,565	46,515	1,268,000
Central City	27,950	2,080	30,030	332,000
Suburban	0	16,485	16,485	936,000
Orlando				
Total	10,378	4,845	15,223	428,000
Central City	8,122	1,402	9,524	98,000
Suburban	2,256	3,443	5,699	330,000
Tampa–St. Petersburg				
Total	31,577	3,910	35,487	1,013,000
Central City	31,577	3,467	35,044	488,000
Suburban	0	443	443	525,000
GEORGIA				
Atlanta				
Total	33,149	13,734	46,883	1,390,000
Central City	22,813	12,658	35,471	488,000
Suburban	10,336	1,076	11,412	902,000
HAWAII				
Honolulu				
Total	29,533	3,340	32,873	631,000
Central City	25,064	2,033	27,097	320,000
Suburban	4,469	1,307	5,776	311,000
ILLINOIS				
Chicago				
Total	125,725	110,250	235,975	6,979,000
Central City	71,302	71,827	143,129	3,323,000
Suburban	54,423	38,423	92,846	3,656,000
Peoria				
Total	6,122	6,330	12,452	342,000
Central City	0	5,789	5,789	126,000
Suburban	6,122	541	6,663	216,000

Standard metropolitan statistical area	Higher education enrollment			Population
	Public	Private	Total	
INDIANA				
Gary–Hammond–East Chicago				
Total	9,156	6,247	15,403	633,000
Central City	9,156	1,605	10,761	328,000
Suburban	0	4,642	4,642	305,000
Indianapolis				
Total	14,605	8,945	23,550	1,110,000
Central City	14,605	8,166	22,771	743,000
Suburban	0	779	779	367,000
IOWA (ILL.)				
Davenport–Rock Island–Moline				
Total	3,762	5,225	8,987	363,000
Central City	3,762	5,225	8,987	192,000
Suburban	0	0	0	171,000
KANSAS				
Wichita				
Total	14,116	1,657	15,773	389,000
Central City	12,395	1,657	14,052	274,000
Suburban	1,721	0	1,721	115,000
KENTUCKY (IND.)				
Louisville				
Total	12,076	3,962	16,038	827,000
Central City	9,668	3,962	13,630	357,000
Suburban	2,408	0	2,408	470,000
LOUISIANA				
New Orleans				
Total	18,258	17,725	35,983	1,046,000
Central City	17,971	17,620	35,591	586,000
Suburban	287	105	392	460,000
MARYLAND				
Baltimore				
Total	47,087	25,493	72,580	2,071,000
Central City	26,385	21,939	48,324	895,000
Suburban	20,702	3,554	24,256	1,176,000

	Higher education enrollment			
Standard metropolitan statistical area	*Public*	*Private*	*Total*	*Population*
MASSACHUSETTS				
Boston				
Total	40,050	146,137	186,187	2,754,000
Central City	26,901	87,336	114,237	628,000
Suburban	13,149	58,801	71,950	2,126,000
Springfield-Chicopee-Holyoke				
Total	10,297	15,131	25,428	530,000
Central City	6,700	9,690	16,390	278,000
Suburban	3,597	5,441	9,038	252,000
Worcester				
Total	11,585	13,448	25,033	344,000
Central City	11,585	12,511	24,096	175,000
Suburban	0	937	937	169,000
MICHIGAN				
Detroit				
Total	131,621	26,044	157,665	4,200,000
Central City	66,190	16,371	82,561	1,493,000
Suburban	65,431	9,673	75,104	2,707,000
Flint				
Total	10,478	3,075	13,553	497,000
Central City	10,478	3,075	13,553	194,000
Suburban	0	0	0	303,000
Grand Rapids				
Total	8,658	7,406	16,064	539,000
Central City	5,357	7,283	12,640	196,000
Suburban	3,301	123	3,424	343,000
Lansing				
Total	51,334	945	52,279	378,000
Central City	51,334	39	51,373	129,000
Suburban	0	906	906	249,000
MINNESOTA				
Minneapolis–St. Paul				
Total	71,552	17,373	88,925	1,814,000
Central City	62,286	14,667	76,953	741,000
Suburban	9,266	2,706	11,972	1,073,000

Standard metropolitan statistical area	Higher education enrollment			Population
	Public	Private	Total	
MISSOURI				
Kansas City (Kans.)				
Total	21,225	8,353	29,578	1,257,000
Central City	15,265	5,405	20,670	662,000
Suburban	5,960	2,948	8,908	595,000
St. Louis (Ill.)				
Total	49,815	27,534	77,349	2,363,000
Central City	29,858	24,228	54,086	608,000
Suburban	19,957	3,306	23,263	1,755,000
NEBRASKA				
Omaha (Iowa)				
Total	14,852	5,962	20,814	541,000
Central City	14,085	5,201	19,286	328,000
Suburban	767	761	1,528	213,000
NEW JERSEY				
Jersey City				
Total	9,834	7,411	17,245	609,000
Central City	9,834	4,761	14,595	253,000
Suburban	0	2,650	2,650	356,000
Newark				
Total	43,135	23,392	66,527	1,857,000
Central City	16,695	621	17,316	378,000
Suburban	26,440	22,771	49,211	1,479,000
Paterson-Clifton-Passaic				
Total	11,230	18,789	30,019	1,359,000
Central City	0	0	0	278,000
Suburban	11,230	18,789	30,019	1,081,000
Trenton				
Total	14,575	12,268	26,843	304,000
Central City	14,575	6,123	20,698	102,000
Suburban	0	6,145	6,145	202,000
NEW MEXICO				
Albuquerque				
Total	18,107	1,563	19,670	316,000

Standard metropolitan statistical area	Higher education enrollment			Population
	Public	*Private*	*Total*	
Central City	18,107	1,563	19,670	244,000
Suburban	0	0	0	72,000
NEW YORK				
Albany-Schenectady-Troy				
Total	20,877	19,612	40,489	721,000
Central City	20,877	15,856	36,733	253,000
Suburban	0	3,756	3,756	468,000
Binghamton (Pa.)				
Total	11,379	0	11,379	303,000
Central City	7,182	0	7,182	63,000
Suburban	4,197	0	4,197	240,000
Buffalo				
Total	43,860	11,924	55,784	1,349,000
Central City	40,755	7,708	48,463	458,000
Suburban	3,105	4,216	7,321	891,000
New York City				
Total	245,277	192,595	437,872	11,529,000
Central City	95,324	102,646	197,970	7,799,000
Suburban	149,953	89,949	239,902	3,730,000
Rochester				
Total	21,980	23,365	45,345	883,000
Central City	8,400	22,629	31,029	294,000
Suburban	13,580	736	14,316	589,000
Syracuse				
Total	16,744	20,274	37,018	636,000
Central City	6,224	17,530	23,754	193,000
Suburban	10,520	2,744	13,264	443,000
Utica-Rome				
Total	4,774	4,683	9,457	340,000
Central City	3,992	3,278	7,270	139,000
Suburban	782	1,405	2,187	201,000
NORTH CAROLINA				
Charlotte				
Total	14,155	6,031	20,186	409,000
Central City	12,103	2,312	14,415	239,000
Suburban	2,052	3,719	5,771	170,000

Standard metropolitan statistical area	Higher education enrollment			Population
	Public	*Private*	*Total*	
Greensboro–Winston-Salem–High Point				
Total	15,029	8,301	23,330	604,000
Central City	13,280	8,248	21,528	328,000
Suburban	1,749	53	1,802	276,000
OHIO				
Akron				
Total	39,459	1,191	40,650	679,000
Central City	18,467	0	18,467	275,000
Suburban	20,992	1,191	22,183	404,000
Canton				
Total	2,519	3,122	5,641	372,000
Central City	2,519	1,854	4,373	109,000
Suburban	0	1,268	1,268	363,000
Cincinnati (Ky./Ind.)				
Total	34,500	9,214	43,714	1,385,000
Central City	32,425	8,308	40,762	448,000
Suburban	2,046	906	2,952	937,000
Cleveland				
Total	34,153	22,105	56,258	2,064,000
Central City	30,563	17,815	48,378	739,000
Suburban	3,590	4,290	7,880	1,325,000
Columbus				
Total	47,897	12,433	60,330	916,000
Central City	47,897	7,994	55,891	533,000
Suburban	0	4,439	4,439	383,000
Dayton				
Total	17,426	18,144	35,570	850,000
Central City	14,146	13,509	27,655	240,000
Suburban	3,280	4,635	7,915	610,000
Toledo (Mich.)				
Total	32,557	1,024	33,581	693,000
Central City	14,958	928	15,886	379,000
Suburban	17,599	96	17,695	314,000
Youngstown-Warren				
Total	16,044	0	16,044	536,000

Standard metropolitan statistical area	Higher education enrollment			Population
	Public	Private	Total	
Central City	15,030	0	15,030	204,000
Suburban	1,014	0	1,014	332,000
OKLAHOMA				
Oklahoma City				
Total	34,147	5,775	39,922	641,000
Central City	2,411	4,055	6,466	363,000
Suburban	31,736	1,720	33,456	278,000
Tulsa				
Total	0	8,054	8,054	476,000
Central City	0	8,054	8,054	328,000
Suburban	0	0	0	148,000
OREGON				
Portland (Wash.)				
Total	38,013	9,069	47,082	1,009,000
Central City	25,046	7,221	32,267	375,000
Suburban	12,967	1,848	14,815	634,000
PENNSYLVANIA				
Allentown-Bethlehem-Easton (N.J.)				
Total	5,432	13,001	18,433	544,000
Central City	5,432	11,768	17,200	210,000
Suburban	0	1,233	1,233	334,000
Harrisburg				
Total	10,643	2,669	13,312	411,000
Central City	3,799	0	3,799	66,000
Suburban	6,844	2,669	9,513	345,000
Lancaster				
Total	5,387	4,806	10,193	320,000
Central City	0	3,099	3,099	58,000
Suburban	5,387	1,707	7,094	262,000
Philadelphia (N.J.)				
Total	111,121	87,202	198,323	4,818,000
Central City	37,244	58,588	95,832	1,928,000
Suburban	73,877	28,614	102,491	2,890,000
Pittsburgh				
Total	50,445	25,808	76,253	2,401,000

Standard metropolitan statistical area	Higher education enrollment			Population
	Public	*Private*	*Total*	
Central City	34,287	22,132	56,419	513,000
Suburban	16,158	3,676	19,834	1,888,000
Wilkes-Barre–Hazleton				
Total	2,275	6,899	9,624	342,000
Central City	2,275	5,958	8,683	88,000
Suburban	0	941	941	254,000
RHODE ISLAND				
Providence-Pawtucket-Warwick (Mass.)				
Total	25,061	20,973	46,034	914,000
Central City	9,995	17,216	27,211	336,000
Suburban	15,066	3,757	18,823	578,000
SOUTH CAROLINA				
Charleston				
Total	5,304	3,368	8,672	304,000
Central City	5,304	3,368	8,672	65,000
Suburban	0	0	0	239,000
Columbia				
Total	15,410	4,149	19,559	323,000
Central City	15,410	4,149	19,559	112,000
Suburban	0	0	0	211,000
Greenville				
Total	9,087	6,699	15,786	300,000
Central City	1,622	5,868	7,490	61,000
Suburban	7,465	831	8,296	239,000
TENNESSEE				
Chattanooga (Ga.)				
Total	5,597	2,844	8,441	305,000
Central City	5,597	1,512	7,109	113,000
Suburban	0	1,332	1,332	192,000
Knoxville				
Total	27,723	2,315	30,038	400,000
Central City	27,723	1,547	29,270	170,000
Suburban	0	768	768	230,000
Memphis (Ark.)				
Total	22,181	9,943	32,124	770,000

Standard metropolitan statistical area	Higher education enrollment			Population
	Public	*Private*	*Total*	
Central City	22,181	9,943	32,124	621,000
Suburban	0	0	0	149,000
Nashville				
Total	4,786	8,975	13,761	541,000
Central City	4,786	8,614	13,400	444,000
Suburban	0	361	361	97,000
TEXAS				
Beaumont–Port Arthur–Orange				
Total	10,874	0	10,874	316,000
Central City	10,874	0	10,874	196,000
Suburban	0	0	0	120,000
Dallas				
Total	34,300	16,739	51,039	1,556,000
Central City	12,816	14,190	27,006	836,000
Suburban	21,484	2,549	24,033	720,000
El Paso				
Total	11,484	0	11,484	359,000
Central City	11,484	0	11,484	317,000
Suburban	0	0	0	42,000
Fort Worth				
Total	24,768	10,557	35,325	762,000
Central City	6,083	10,142	16,225	388,000
Suburban	18,685	415	19,100	374,000
Houston				
Total	52,021	11,858	63,879	1,985,000
Central City	31,816	11,858	43,674	1,213,000
Suburban	20,205	0	20,205	772,000
San Antonio				
Total	14,844	11,298	26,142	864,000
Central City	14,844	10,314	25,158	650,000
Suburban	0	984	984	214,000
UTAH				
Salt Lake City				
Total	23,390	2,524	25,914	558,000

Standard metropolitan statistical area	Higher education enrollment			Population
	Public	Private	Total	
Central City	23,390	2,524	25,914	177,000
Suburban	0	0	0	381,000
VIRGINIA				
Norfolk-Portsmouth				
Total	11,934	634	12,568	681,000
Central City	11,934	634	12,568	378,000
Suburban	0	0	0	303,000
Richmond				
Total	16,063	7,020	23,083	518,000
Central City	14,211	6,220	20,431	248,000
Suburban	1,852	800	2,652	270,000
WASHINGTON				
Seattle-Everett				
Total	67,270	5,974	73,244	1,422,000
Central City	53,641	5,382	59,023	576,000
Suburban	13,629	592	14,221	846,000
Tacoma				
Total	5,695	6,664	12,359	411,000
Central City	5,695	6,664	12,359	151,000
Suburban	0	0	0	260,000
WISCONSIN				
Milwaukee				
Total	37,245	18,124	55,369	1,404,000
Central City	37,245	16,749	53,994	710,000
Suburban	0	1,375	1,375	694,000

SOURCE: Prepared by Carnegie Commission staff from data in U.S. Office of Education: *Opening Fall Enrollment in Higher Education, 1970, Supplementary Information, Institutional Data*, Washington, D.C., 1971.

Appendix B: Higher Education Enrollment in Metropolitan Areas

	(1) Enrollment as a percentage of population			(2) Proportion of out-of-state enrollment	(3) Column (1) modified by column (2)
	Public	Private	Total		
ALABAMA					
Birmingham					
Total	1.93%	0.81%	2.74%	8.22%	2.51%
Central City	3.97	1.77	5.74	9.72	5.18
Suburban	0.56	0.17	0.72	3.87	0.69
Mobile					
Total	1.92	0.37	2.28	4.44	2.18
Central City	3.26	0.74	4.00	4.84	3.81
Suburban	0.58	0.00	0.58	2.68	0.56
ARIZONA					
Phoenix					
Total	6.05	0.19	6.25	9.05	5.68
Central City	2.62	0.32	2.94	2.53	2.87
Suburban	11.19	0.00	11.19	11.95	9.85
Tucson					
Total	8.41	0.00	8.41	25.57	6.26
Central City	11.47	0.00	11.47	25.57	8.54
Suburban	0.00	0.00	0.00	0.00	0.00
ARKANSAS					
Little Rock–North Little Rock					
Total	1.50	0.40	1.89	4.09	1.81
Central City	2.57	0.68	3.25	4.09	3.12
Suburban	0.00	0.00	0.00	0.00	0.00

	(1) Enrollment as a percentage of population			(2) Proportion of out-of-state enrollment	(3) Column (1) modified by column (2)
	Public	Private	Total		
CALIFORNIA					
Anaheim–Santa Ana–Garden Grove					
Total	4.74%	0.50%	5.24%	4.56%	5.00%
Central City	3.40	0.00	3.40	1.91	4.92
Suburban	5.34	0.73	6.07	4.75	5.78
Bakersfield					
Total	3.62	0.00	3.62	2.36	3.53
Central City	16.56	0.00	16.56	1.33	16.34
Suburban	0.25	0.00	0.25	10.60	0.22
Fresno					
Total	7.97	0.13	8.10	2.92	7.86
Central City	18.12	0.32	18.44	2.68	17.95
Suburban	1.42	0.00	1.42	5.70	1.34
Los Angeles–Long Beach					
Total	5.01	0.77	5.78	5.48	5.46
Central City	5.40	1.41	6.81	5.69	12.66
Suburban	4.71	0.30	5.01	5.30	4.74
Oxnard–Ventura					
Total	3.70	0.36	4.07	3.66	3.92
Central City	6.52	0.00	6.52	1.91	6.40
Suburban	2.27	0.55	2.82	10.63	2.52
Sacramento					
Total	7.99	0.00	7.99	2.17	7.82
Central City	18.11	0.00	18.11	2.24	17.70
Suburban	3.20	0.00	3.20	1.29	3.16
San Bernardino–Riverside–Ontario					
Total	4.22	0.77	5.00	13.50	4.33
Central City	10.27	0.22	10.49	14.69	8.95
Suburban	1.97	0.97	2.94	12.49	2.57
San Diego					
Total	6.43	0.46	6.89	2.68	6.71
Central City	9.47	0.93	10.20	2.69	9.93
Suburban	3.61	0.00	3.61	2.63	3.52
San Francisco–Oakland					
Total	5.63	0.74	6.37	3.77	6.13

	(1) Enrollment as a percentage of population			(2) Proportion of out-of-state enrollment	(3) Column (1) modified by column (2)
	Public	Private	Total		
Central City	6.18%	1.57%	7.75%	5.34%	7.34%
Suburban	5.35	0.31	5.66	2.57	5.51
San Jose					
Total	6.66	1.75	8.40	7.27	7.79
Central City	10.92	0.06	10.99	2.18	10.75
Suburban	3.69	2.92	6.60	13.13	5.73
COLORADO					
Denver					
Total	3.78	1.05	4.64	46.36	2.49
Central City	3.77	2.50	6.28	51.36	3.05
Suburban	3.80	0.00	3.80	20.11	3.04
CONNECTICUT					
Bridgeport					
Total	1.96	3.96	5.92	30.72	4.10
Central City	3.49	7.48	10.97	29.87	7.69
Suburban	0.94	1.63	2.57	33.96	1.70
Hartford					
Total	2.71	2.01	4.72	16.03	3.96
Central City	9.81	1.49	11.29	17.26	9.34
Suburban	0.53	2.17	2.70	14.71	2.30
New Haven					
Total	5.47	5.08	10.55	18.36	8.61
Central City	12.29	7.67	19.97	22.75	15.43
Suburban	1.36	3.51	4.87	10.12	4.38
DELAWARE (N.J./MD.)					
Wilmington					
Total	3.65	0.56	4.21	31.68*	
Central City	2.58	2.98	5.56	n.a.	
Suburban	3.86	0.10	4.04	19.32	
DISTRICT OF COLUMBIA (MD./VA.)					
Washington, D.C.					
Total	3.04	2.36	5.40	44.12*	
Central City	1.41	8.83	10.24	67.11	
Suburban	3.62	0.08	3.70	23.35	

	(1) Enrollment as a percentage of population			(2) Proportion of out-of-state enrollment	(3) Column (1) modified by column (2)
	Public	Private	Total		
FLORIDA					
Fort Lauderdale–Hollywood					
Total	1.14%	0.15%	1.30%	19.47%	1.05%
Central City	2.91	0.38	3.29	19.47	2.65
Suburban	0.00	0.00	0.00	0.00	0.00
Jacksonville					
Total	1.26	1.06	2.32	12.53	2.03
Central City	1.30	1.09	2.39	12.53	2.09
Suburban	0.00	0.00	0.00	0.00	0.00
Miami					
Total	2.20	1.46	3.66	26.60	2.69
Central City	8.42	0.62	9.04	10.93	8.05
Suburban	0.00	1.76	1.76	50.03	0.88
Orlando					
Total	2.42	1.13	3.56	2.39	3.47
Central City	8.29	1.43	9.72	2.83	9.44
Suburban	0.68	1.04	1.73	1.30	1.71
Tampa–St. Petersburg					
Total	3.12	0.39	3.50	13.07	3.04
Central City	6.47	0.71	7.18	12.12	6.31
Suburban	0.00	0.08	0.08	68.41	0.03
GEORGIA					
Atlanta					
Total	2.38	0.98	3.37	16.34	2.82
Central City	4.68	2.59	7.26	17.53	5.99
Suburban	1.14	0.11	1.26	13.40	1.09
HAWAII					
Honolulu					
Total	4.68	0.52	5.20	25.57	3.87
Central City	7.83	0.63	8.46	28.60	6.04
Suburban	1.44	0.42	1.86	23.09	1.43
ILLINOIS					
Chicago					
Total	1.80	1.57	3.38	17.10	2.80

	(1) Enrollment as a percentage of population			(2) Proportion of out-of-state enrollment	(3) Column (1) modified by column (2)
	Public	Private	Total		
Central City	2.14%	2.16%	4.30%	14.29%	3.69%
Suburban	1.48	1.05	2.53	19.89	2.03
Peoria					
Total	1.79	1.85	3.64	22.19	2.83
Central City	0.00	4.59	4.59	26.39	3.38
Suburban	2.83	0.25	3.09	7.64	2.85
INDIANA					
Gary–Hammond–East Chicago					
Total	1.45	0.98	2.43	75.86	0.59
Central City	2.79	0.49	3.28	0.00	3.28
Suburban	0.00	1.52	1.52	75.86	0.37
Indianapolis					
Total	1.32	0.80	2.12	25.41	1.58
Central City	1.97	1.09	3.06	21.70	2.40
Suburban	0.00	0.21	0.21	55.98	0.09
IOWA (ILL.)					
Davenport–Rock Island–Moline					
Total	1.03	1.44	2.47	35.59*	
Central City	1.95	2.72	4.68	34.59*	
Suburban	0.00	0.00	0.00	0.00	
KANSAS					
Wichita					
Total	3.63	0.42	4.05	6.52	3.64
Central City	4.52	0.60	5.12	7.30	4.53
Suburban	1.50	0.00	1.50	1.88	1.47
KENTUCKY (IND.)					
Louisville					
Total	1.46	0.47	1.93	13.31*	
Central City	2.71	1.10	3.81	13.31	
Suburban	0.51	0.00	0.51	0.00	
LOUISIANA					
New Orleans					
Total	1.75	1.69	3.44	30.55	2.39

	(1) Enrollment as a percentage of population			(2) Proportion of out-of-state enrollment	(3) Column (1) modified by column (2)
	Public	Private	Total		
Central City	3.07%	3.01%	6.07%	30.55%	4.22%
Suburban	0.06	0.02	0.07	0.00	0.07
MARYLAND					
Baltimore					
Total	2.27	1.23	3.50	10.84	3.12
Central City	2.95	2.45	5.40	9.24	4.90
Suburban	1.76	0.30	2.06	15.33	1.74
MASSACHUSETTS					
Boston					
Total	1.45	5.31	6.76	33.15	4.52
Central City	4.28	13.91	18.19	26.71	13.33
Suburban	0.62	2.77	3.38	44.80	1.87
Springfield-Chicopee-Holyoke					
Total	1.94	2.86	4.80	35.98	3.07
Central City	2.41	3.49	5.90	24.03	4.48
Suburban	1.43	2.16	3.59	52.20	1.72
Worcester					
Total	3.37	3.91	7.28	25.73	5.41
Central City	6.62	7.15	13.77	25.13	10.31
Suburban	0.00	0.55	0.55	35.68	0.35
MICHIGAN					
Detroit					
Total	3.13	0.62	3.75	6.22	3.52
Central City	4.38	1.10	5.53	7.32	5.13
Suburban	2.42	0.36	2.77	5.27	2.62
Flint					
Total	2.11	0.62	2.73	31.41	1.87
Central City	5.40	1.59	6.99	31.41	4.79
Suburban	0.00	0.00	0.00	0.00	0.00
Grand Rapids					
Total	1.61	1.37	2.98	15.86	2.51
Central City	2.73	3.72	6.45	18.87	5.23
Suburban	0.96	0.04	1.00	2.14	0.98

	(1) Enrollment as a percentage of population			(2) Proportion of out-of-state enrollment	(3) Column (1) modified by column (2)
	Public	Private	Total		
Lansing					
Total	13.58%	0.25%	13.83%	4.81%	13.16%
Central City	39.79	0.03	39.82	2.22	38.94
Suburban	0.00	0.36	0.36	17.86	0.30
MINNESOTA					
Minneapolis–St. Paul					
Total	3.94	0.96	4.90	26.06	3.62
Central City	8.41	1.98	10.39	30.50	7.22
Suburban	0.86	0.25	1.12	18.78	0.91
MISSOURI					
Kansas City (Kans.)					
Total	1.69	0.66	2.35	26.36*	
Central City	2.31	0.82	3.12	29.79	
Suburban	1.00	0.50	1.50	20.23	
St. Louis (Ill.)					
Total	2.11	1.17	3.27	32.10*	
Central City	4.91	3.98	8.90	40.62	
Suburban	1.14	0.19	1.33	20.20	
NEBRASKA					
Omaha (Iowa)					
Total	2.75	1.10	3.85	54.76*	
Central City	4.29	1.59	5.88	54.76	
Suburban	0.36	0.36	0.72	0.00	
NEW JERSEY					
Jersey City					
Total	1.62	1.22	2.84	6.98	2.64
Central City	3.89	1.88	5.77	3.39	5.57
Suburban	0.00	0.74	0.74	35.32	0.48
Newark					
Total	2.32	1.26	3.58	6.54	3.35
Central City	4.42	0.16	4.58	6.10	4.30
Suburban	1.79	1.54	3.33	6.63	3.11

	(1) Enrollment as a percentage of population			(2) Proportion of out-of-state enrollment	(3) Column (1) modified by column (2)
	Public	Private	Total		
Paterson-Clifton-Passaic					
Total	0.83%	1.38%	2.23%	3.60%	2.15%
Central City	0.00	0.00	0.00	0.00	0.00
Suburban	1.04	1.74	2.78	3.60	2.68
Trenton					
Total	4.79	4.04	8.83	30.50	6.14
Central City	14.29	6.00	20.29	17.25	16.79
Suburban	0.00	3.04	3.04	84.70	0.47
NEW MEXICO					
Albuquerque					
Total	5.73	0.50	6.23	14.75	5.31
Central City	7.42	0.64	8.06	14.75	6.87
Suburban	0.00	0.00	0.00	0.00	0.00
NEW YORK					
Albany-Schenectady-Troy					
Total	2.90	2.72	5.62	5.17	5.33
Central City	8.25	6.27	14.52	4.42	13.88
Suburban	0.00	0.80	0.80	11.96	0.70
Binghamton (Pa.)					
Total	3.76	0.00	3.76	3.42*	
Central City	11.40	0.00	11.40	3.02	
Suburban	1.75	0.00	1.75	3.80	
Buffalo					
Total	3.25	0.88	4.14	2.49	4.04
Central City	8.90	1.68	10.58	2.66	10.30
Suburban	0.35	0.47	0.82	0.55	0.82
New York City					
Total	2.13	1.67	3.80	7.44	3.52
Central City	1.22	1.32	2.54	10.69	2.27
Suburban	4.02	2.41	6.43	5.37	6.08
Rochester					
Total	2.49	2.65	5.14	8.82	4.69

	(1) Enrollment as a percentage of population			(2) Proportion of out-of-state enrollment	(3) Column (1) modified by column (2)
	Public	*Private*	*Total*		
Central City	2.86%	7.70 %	10.55%	10.63%	9.43%
Suburban	2.31	0.13	2.43	3.64	2.34
Syracuse					
Total	2.63	3.19	5.82	10.04	5.24
Central City	3.23	9.08	12.31	4.92	11.70
Suburban	2.38	0.62	2.99	13.48	2.59
Utica-Rome					
Total	1.40	1.38	2.78	8.88	2.48
Central City	2.87	2.36	5.23	0.73	5.19
Suburban	0.39	0.70	1.09	25.92	0.81
NORTH CAROLINA					
Charlotte					
Total	3.46	1.48	4.94	26.42	3.63
Central City	5.06	0.97	6.03	26.57	4.43
Suburban	1.21	2.19	3.40	26.30	2.51
Greensboro–Winston-Salem– *High Point*					
Total	2.49	1.37	3.86	29.82	2.71
Central City	4.05	2.52	6.56	29.80	4.61
Suburban	0.63	0.02	0.65	34.18	0.43
OHIO					
Akron					
Total	5.81	0.18	5.99	8.38	5.49
Central City	6.72	0.00	6.72	5.13	6.38
Suburban	5.20	0.30	5.49	44.41	3.05
Canton					
Total	0.68	0.84	1.52	18.63	1.24
Central City	2.31	1.70	4.01	16.62	3.34
Suburban	0.00	0.48	0.48	22.02	0.37
Cincinnati (Ky., Ind.)					
Total	2.49	0.67	3.16	25.03*	
Central City	7.24	1.85	9.10	25.58	
Suburban	0.22	0.10	0.32	22.39	

	(1) Enrollment as a percentage of population			(2) Proportion of out-of-state enrollment	(3) Column (1) modified by column (2)
	Public	*Private*	*Total*		
Cleveland					
Total	1.66%	1.07%	2.73%	17.24%	2.26%
Central City	4.14	2.41	6.55	15.33	5.55
Suburban	0.27	0.32	0.59	26.83	0.43
Columbus					
Total	5.23	1.36	6.59	25.19	4.93
Central City	8.99	1.50	10.49	10.24	9.42
Suburban	0.00	1.16	1.16	48.13	0.60
Dayton					
Total	2.05	2.11	4.16	36.55	2.64
Central City	5.89	5.54	11.43	33.95	7.55
Suburban	0.54	0.76	1.30	45.34	0.71
Toledo (Mich.)					
Total	4.70	0.15	4.85	10.35*	
Central City	3.94	0.25	4.19	10.89	
Suburban	5.60	0.03	5.64	5.80	
Youngstown-Warren					
Total	2.99	0.00	2.99	22.96	2.30
Central City	7.37	0.00	7.37	22.96	5.68
Suburban	0.00	0.00	0.00	0.00	0.00
OKLAHOMA					
Oklahoma City					
Total	5.33	0.90	6.23	16.78	5.18
Central City	0.66	1.12	1.78	27.91	1.28
Suburban	11.42	0.62	12.04	13.22	10.45
Tulsa					
Total	0.00	1.69	1.69	20.40	1.35
Central City	0.00	2.46	2.46	20.40	1.96
Suburban	0.00	0.00	0.00	0.00	0.00
OREGON					
Portland (Wash.)					
Total	3.77	0.90	4.67	18.74*	
Central City	6.68	1.93	8.60	20.65	
Suburban	2.05	0.29	2.34	13.13	

	(1) Enrollment as a percentage of population			(2) Proportion of out-of-state enrollment	(3) Column (1) modified by column (2)
	Public	Private	Total		

PENNSYLVANIA

Allentown-Bethlehem-Easton (N.J.)

Total	1.00%	2.39%	3.39%	41.38%*	
Central City	2.59	5.60	8.19	42.17	
Suburban	0.00	0.37	0.37	22.58	

Harrisburg

Total	2.59	0.65	3.24	14.12	2.78%
Central City	5.76	0.00	5.76	0.30	5.74
Suburban	1.98	0.77	2.76	18.98	2.24

Lancaster

Total	1.68	1.50	3.19	18.45	2.60
Central City	0.00	5.34	5.34	44.13	2.98
Suburban	2.06	0.65	2.71	7.15	2.52

Philadelphia

Total	2.31	1.81	4.12	22.47	3.19
Central City	1.93	3.04	4.97	21.88	3.88
Suburban	2.56	0.99	3.55	23.35	2.72

Pittsburgh

Total	2.10	1.07	3.18	15.74	2.68
Central City	6.68	4.31	11.00	21.08	8.68
Suburban	0.86	0.20	1.05	8.14	0.96

Wilkes-Barre–Hazleton

Total	0.80	2.02	2.81	17.77	2.31
Central City	3.10	6.77	9.87	16.34	8.26
Suburban	0.00	0.37	0.37	25.48	0.28

RHODE ISLAND

Providence-Pawtucket-Warwick (R.I., Mass.)

Total	2.74	2.30	5.04	42.26*	
Central City	2.98	5.12	8.10	40.25	
Suburban	2.61	0.65	3.26	67.57	

SOUTH CAROLINA

Charleston

Total	1.75	1.11	2.85	34.59	1.86

	(1) Enrollment as a percentage of population			(2) Proportion of out-of-state enrollment	(3) Column (1) modified by column (2)
	Public	Private	Total		
Central City	8.16%	5.18%	13.34%	34.59%	8.73%
Suburban	0.00	0.00	0.00	0.00	0.00
Columbia					
Total	4.77	1.28	6.06	25.08	4.54
Central City	13.76	3.70	17.46	25.08	13.08
Suburban	0.00	0.00	0.00	0.00	0.00
Greenville					
Total	3.03	2.23	5.26	43.23	2.99
Central City	2.66	9.61	12.28	52.63	5.82
Suburban	3.12	0.35	3.47	7.24	3.22
TENNESSEE					
Chattanooga (Ga.)					
Total	1.84	0.93	2.77	52.21*	
Central City	4.95	1.34	6.29	46.00	
Suburban	0.00	0.69	0.69	69.92	
Knoxville					
Total	6.93	0.58	7.51	69.26	2.31
Central City	16.31	0.91	17.22	69.26	5.29
Suburban	0.00	0.33	0.33	0.00	0.33
Memphis (Ark.)					
Total	2.88	1.29	4.17	27.78*	
Central City	3.57	1.60	5.17	27.78	
Suburban	0.00	0.00	0.00	0.00	
Nashville					
Total	0.88	1.66	2.54	44.08	1.42
Central City	1.08	1.94	3.02	45.10	1.66
Suburban	0.00	0.37	0.37	14.91	0.31
TEXAS					
Beaumont–Port Arthur–Orange					
Total	3.44	0.00	3.44	2.87	3.34
Central City	5.55	0.00	5.55	2.87	5.39
Suburban	0.00	0.00	0.00	0.00	0.00

	(1) Enrollment as a percentage of population			(2) Proportion of out-of-state enrollment	(3) Column (1) modified by column (2)
	Public	*Private*	*Total*		
Dallas					
Total	2.20%	1.08%	3.28%	14.97%	2.79%
Central City	1.53	1.70	3.23	18.62	2.63
Suburban	2.98	0.35	3.34	12.06	2.94
El Paso					
Total	3.12	0.00	3.12	16.19	2.61
Central City	3.62	0.00	3.62	16.19	3.03
Suburban	0.00	0.00	0.00	0.00	0.00
Fort Worth					
Total	3.25	1.39	4.64	7.20	4.31
Central City	1.57	2.61	4.18	12.53	3.66
Suburban	5.00	0.11	5.11	3.87	4.91
Houston					
Total	2.62	0.60	3.22	7.72	2.97
Central City	2.62	0.98	3.60	9.48	3.26
Suburban	2.62	0.00	2.62	3.18	2.54
San Antonio					
Total	1.72	1.31	3.03	13.70	2.61
Central City	2.28	1.59	3.87	13.70	3.34
Suburban	0.00	0.46	0.46	0.00	0.46
UTAH					
Salt Lake City					
Total	4.19	0.45	4.64	11.60	4.10
Central City	13.21	1.43	14.64	11.60	12.94
Suburban	0.00	0.00	0.00	0.00	0.00
VIRGINIA					
Norfolk-Portsmouth					
Total	1.75	0.09	1.85	10.76	1.65
Central City	3.16	0.17	3.33	10.76	2.97
Suburban	0.00	0.00	0.00	0.00	0.00
Richmond					
Total	3.10	1.36	4.46	18.03	3.66
Central City	5.73	2.51	8.24	16.66	6.87
Suburban	0.69	0.30	0.98	22.89	0.76

	(1) Enrollment as a percentage of population			(2) Proportion of out-of-state enrollment	(3) Column (1) modified by column (2)
	Public	*Private*	*Total*		
WASHINGTON					
Seattle-Everett					
Total	4.73%	0.42%	5.15%	11.81%	4.54%
Central City	9.31	0.93	10.25	12.14	9.01
Suburban	1.61	0.06	1.68	10.34	1.51
Tacoma					
Total	1.39	1.62	3.01	18.23	2.46
Central City	3.77	4.41	8.19	18.23	6.70
Suburban	0.00	0.00	0.00	0.00	0.00
WISCONSIN					
Milwaukee					
Total	2.65	1.29	3.94	19.91	3.16
Central City	5.25	2.36	7.60	18.56	6.19
Suburban	0.00	0.20	0.20	30.69	0.14

*These figures are not as meaningful for these areas because more than one state is included within the boundaries of the metropolitan area.

NOTE: n.a. indicates not available.

SOURCE: Prepared by Carnegie Commission staff from data in U.S. Office of Education: *Opening Fall Enrollment in Higher Education, 1970, Supplementary Information, Institutional Data,* Washington, D.C., 1971; U.S. Office of Education, unpublished data on residence and migration of students, Fall 1968.

Appendix C: Enrollment Patterns in Metropolitan Areas

	Enrollment in public colleges and universities				Enrollment in private colleges and universities			
	Two-year colleges	Comprehensive colleges & universities	Doctoral-granting institutions	Professional & specialized institutions	Two-year colleges	Liberal arts colleges	Doctoral-granting institutions	Professional & specialized institutions
ALABAMA								
Birmingham								
Central City	29.44%	28.85%	0.00%	0.00%	0.00%	25.03%	0.00%	0.92%
Suburban	0.00	12.13	0.00	0.00	3.62	0.00	0.00	0.00
Mobile								
Central City	10.61	60.59	0.00	0.00	0.00	16.17	0.00	0.00
Suburban	12.60	0.00	0.00	0.00	0.00	0.00	0.00	0.00
ARIZONA								
Phoenix								
Central City	25.13	0.00	0.00	0.00	0.00	1.40	0.00	1.66
Suburban	22.50	0.00	49.28	0.00	0.00	0.00	0.00	0.00
Tucson								
Central City	11.78	0.00	88.21	0.00	0.00	0.00	100.00	0.00
Suburban	0.00	0.00	0.00	0.00	0.00	0.00	0.00	0.00
ARKANSAS								
Little Rock–North Little Rock								
Central City	0.00	65.37	0.00	13.59	4.33	16.70	0.00	0.00
Suburban	0.00	0.00	0.00	0.00	0.00	0.00	0.00	0.00
CALIFORNIA								
Anaheim–Santa Ana–Garden Grove								
Central City	11.19	0.00	8.94	0.00	0.00	0.00	0.00	0.00

Suburban	49.42	20.87	0.00	0.00	0.00	8.84	0.00	0.72
Bakersfield								
Central City	86.56	7.93	0.00	0.00	0.00	0.00	0.00	0.00
Suburban	5.51	0.00	0.00	0.00	0.00	0.00	0.00	0.00
Fresno								
Central City	37.85	49.93	0.00	0.00	0.00	1.55	0.00	0.00
Suburban	10.67	0.00	0.00	0.00	0.00	0.00	0.00	0.00
Los Angeles–Long Beach								
Central City	20.21	12.75	7.14	0.09	0.00	4.21	5.10	1.19
Suburban	38.13	8.20	0.00	0.00	0.04	1.67	0.57	0.64
Oxnard-Ventura								
Central City	54.10	0.00	0.00	0.00	0.00	0.00	0.00	0.00
Suburban	36.92	0.00	0.00	0.00	0.00	8.96	0.00	0.00
Sacramento								
Central City	42.14	30.75	0.00	0.00	0.00	0.00	0.00	0.00
Suburban	6.24	0.00	20.79	0.00	0.00	0.00	0.00	0.00
San Bernardino–Riverside–Ontario								
Central City	40.38	4.91	10.50	0.00	0.00	1.21	0.00	0.00
Suburban	28.79	0.00	0.00	0.00	0.00	14.21	0.00	0.00
San Diego								
Central City	23.86	37.18	5.92	0.00	0.00	1.54	4.38	0.76
Suburban	26.32	0.00	0.00	0.00	0.00	0.00	0.00	0.00
San Francisco–Oakland								
Central City	21.98	9.18	0.00	1.96	0.07	6.63	0.00	1.71
Suburban	32.93	7.86	14.38	0.00	0.15	2.22	0.00	0.86

	Enrollment in public colleges and universities				Enrollment in private colleges and universities			
	Two-year colleges	Comprehensive colleges & universities	Doctoral-granting institutions	Professional & specialized institutions	Two-year colleges	Liberal arts colleges	Doctoral-granting institutions	Professional & specialized institutions
CALIFORNIA cont.:								
San Jose								
Central City	15.76%	37.59%	0.00%	0.00%	0.00%	0.00%	0.00%	0.31%
Suburban	25.86	0.00	0.00	0.00	0.00	6.69	13.80	0.00
COLORADO								
Denver								
Central City	6.64	23.28	0.00	2.63	0.00	5.11	15.73	0.84
Suburban	6.69	0.00	36.14	2.90	0.00	0.00	0.00	0.00
CONNECTICUT								
Bridgeport								
Central City	23.54	0.00	0.00	0.00	0.00	47.89	0.00	2.49
Suburban	9.51	0.00	0.00	0.00	0.86	15.70	0.00	0.01
Hartford								
Central City	8.95	39.87	0.00	0.00	1.12	6.28	0.00	0.00
Suburban	8.56	0.00	0.00	0.00	0.11	33.04	0.00	2.06
New Haven								
Central City	10.55	33.32	0.00	0.00	1.96	1.46	23.77	0.19
Suburban	8.01	0.00	0.00	0.00	0.07	20.68	0.00	0.00
DELAWARE								
Wilmington (N.J./Md.)								
Central City	9.83	0.00	0.00	0.00	11.30	0.00	0.00	0.00
Suburban	2.01	0.00	74.71	0.00	0.00	0.00	0.00	0.00

DISTRICT OF COLUMBIA

Washington (Md./Va.)

Central City	1.34	5.45	0.00	0.00	0.49	1.40	38.74	1.98
Suburban	15.82	1.56	29.28	2.83	0.42	0.62	0.00	0.00

FLORIDA

Fort Lauderdale–Hollywood

Central City	88.50	0.00	0.00	0.00	0.00	10.73	0.00	0.78
Suburban	0.00	0.00	0.00	0.00	0.00	0.00	0.00	0.00

Jacksonville

Central City	54.16	0.00	0.00	0.00	0.00	32.95	0.00	12.88
Suburban	0.00	0.00	0.00	0.00	0.00	0.00	0.00	0.00

Miami

Central City	60.09	0.00	0.00	0.00	0.09	4.38	0.00	0.00
Suburban	0.00	0.00	0.00	0.00	0.00	0.96	34.47	0.00

Orlando

Central City	21.13	32.23	0.00	0.00	9.21	0.00	0.00	0.00
Suburban	14.82	0.00	0.00	0.00	0.00	22.62	0.00	0.00

Tampa–St. Petersburg

Central City	38.23	50.75	0.00	0.00	0.00	9.77	0.00	0.00
Suburban	0.00	0.00	0.00	0.00	1.25	0.00	0.00	0.00

GEORGIA

Atlanta

Central City	0.00	30.96	17.68	0.00	0.00	14.87	10.93	1.19
Suburban	22.04	0.00	0.00	0.00	0.00	1.48	0.00	0.81

	Enrollment in public colleges and universities				Enrollment in private colleges and universities			
	Two-year colleges	Comprehensive colleges & universities	Doctoral-granting institutions	Professional & specialized institutions	Two-year colleges	Liberal arts colleges	Doctoral-granting institutions	Professional & specialized institutions
HAWAII								
Honolulu								
Central City	12.59%	0.00%	63.64%	0.00%	0.00%	5.15%	0.00%	1.02%
Suburban	12.63	0.00	0.00	0.00.	0.00	3.97	0.00	0.00
ILLINOIS								
Chicago								
Central City	14.62	14.29	0.00	1.28	2.12	9.01	14.31	4.99
Suburban	23.06	0.00	0.00	0.00	0.51	8.83	6.59	0.32
Peoria								
Central City	0.00	0.00	0.00	.00	0.00	46.49	0.00	0.00
Suburban	49.16	0.00	0.00	0.00	0.00	4.34	0.00	0.00
INDIANA								
Gary–Hammond–East Chicago								
Central City	30.13	29.31	0.00	0.00	0.00	10.42	0.00	0.00
Suburban	0.00	0.00	0.00	0.00	0.00	29.79	0.00	0.33
Indianapolis								
Central City	16.44	0.00	0.00	45.56	0.00	33.39	0.00	1.27
Suburban	0.00	0.00	0.00	0.00	0.00	3.30	0.00	0.00
Davenport–Rock Island–Moline (Ill.)								
Central City	41.86	0.00	0.00	0.00	7.01	58.38	0.00	0.00

	C1	C2	C3	C4	C5	C6	C7	C8
KANSAS								
Wichita								
Central City	0.00	81.97	0.00	0.00	0.00	6.65	0.00	0.00
Suburban	11.38	0.00	0.00	0.00	0.00	0.00	0.00	0.00
KENTUCKY								
Louisville (Ind.)								
Central City	0.00	0.00	60.28	0.00	0.00	17.95	0.00	6.75
Suburban	15.01	0.00	0.00	0.00	0.00	0.00	0.00	0.00
LOUISIANA								
New Orleans								
Central City	11.27	36.30	0.00	2.37	0.00	23.57	23.33	2.07
Suburban	0.79	0.00	0.00	0.00	0.00	0.00	0.00	0.29
MARYLAND								
Baltimore								
Central City	8.77	23.18	0.00	4.39	0.05	13.49	13.41	3.26
Suburban	21.30	7.20	0.00	0.00	0.31	4.58	0.00	0.00
MASSACHUSETTS								
Boston								
Central City	2.14	8.08	0.00	4.24	3.92	6.00	33.90	3.08
Suburban	4.79	2.27	0.00	0.00	1.19	4.97	24.27	1.15
Springfield-Chicopee-Holyoke (Conn.)								
Central City	26.35	0.00	0.00	0.00	0.00	38.11	0.00	0.00
Suburban	0.00	14.15	0.00	0.00	4.10	17.30	0.00	0.00
Worcester								
Central City	12.86	33.42	0.00	0.00	11.16	16.20	12.83	9.79
Suburban	0.00	0.00	0.00	0.00	1.29	2.46	0.00	0.00

	Enrollment in public colleges and universities				Enrollment in private colleges and universities			
	Two-year colleges	*Comprehensive colleges & universities*	*Doctoral-granting institutions*	*Professional & specialized institutions*	*Two-year colleges*	*Liberal arts colleges*	*Doctoral-granting institutions*	*Professional & specialized institutions*
MICHIGAN								
Detroit								
Central City	18.81%	0.55%	22.61%	0.00%	0.00%	8.79%	0.00%	1.58%
Suburban	22.72	18.76	0.00	0.00	0.13	1.95	0.00	4.04
Flint								
Central City	63.66	13.42	0.00	0.00	0.00	0.00	0.00	22.68
Suburban	0.00	0.00	0.00	0.00	0.00	0.00	0.00	0.00
Grand Rapids								
Central City	33.34	0.00	0.00	0.00	8.19	32.23	0.00	6.95
Suburban	0.00	20.54	0.00	0.00	0.00	0.00	0.00	0.76
Lansing								
Central City	13.85	0.00	84.33	0.00	0.00	0.00	0.00	0.07
Suburban	0.00	0.00	0.00	0.00	0.00	1.73	0.00	0.00
MINNESOTA								
Minneapolis–St. Paul								
Central City	1.60	0.00	68.43	0.00	2.25	10.81	0.00	3.41
Suburban	10.41	0.00	0.00	0.00	0.00	2.88	0.00	0.15
MISSOURI								
Kansas City (Kans.)								
Central City	19.17	0.00	32.42	0.00	1.18	10.35	0.00	6.72
Suburban	20.14	0.00	0.00	0.00	2.51	7.45	0.00	0.00

St. Louis (Ill.)								
Central City	23.55	13.17	0.00	1.87	0.95	2.78	26.44	0.86
Suburban	7.35	18.44	0.00	0.00	0.76	3.51	0.00	0.26
NEBRASKA								
Omaha (Iowa)								
Central City	0.00	63.34	0.00	4.34	0.00	22.31	0.00	2.66
Suburban	3.68	0.00	0.00	0.00	0.00	3.65	0.00	0.00
NEW JERSEY								
Jersey City								
Central City	0.00	53.71	0.00	3.30	0.00	27.51	0.00	0.09
Suburban	0.00	0.00	0.00	0.00	0.00	0.00	0.00	15.36
Newark								
Central City	7.38	8.74	0.00	8.96	0.93	0.00	0.00	0.00
Suburban	6.45	33.28	0.00	0.00	4.48	26.98	2.33	0.41
Paterson-Clifton-Passaic								
Central City	0.00	0.00	0.00	0.00	0.00	0.00	0.00	0.00
Suburban	13.62	23.77	0.00	0.00	7.50	54.52	0.00	0.54
Trenton								
Central City	17.40	36.89	0.00	0.00	0.00	22.81	0.00	0.00
Suburban	0.00	0.00	0.00	0.00	0.00	0.00	19.22	3.67
NEW MEXICO								
Albuquerque								
Central City	0.00	0.00	92.05	0.00	0.00	7.95	0.00	0.00
Suburban	0.00	0.00	0.00	0.00	0.00	0.00	0.00	0.00

	Enrollment in public colleges and universities				Enrollment in private colleges and universities			
	Two-year colleges	Comprehensive colleges & universities	Doctoral-granting institutions	Professional & specialized institutions	Two-year colleges	Liberal arts colleges	Doctoral-granting institutions	Professional & specialized institutions
NEW YORK								
Albany-Schenectady-Troy								
Central City	18.74%	0.00%	32.81%	0.00%	2.43%	20.06%	12.52%	16.78%
Suburban	0.00	0.00	0.00	0.00	0.08	9.19	0.00	0.00
Binghamton (Pa.)								
Central City	0.00	63.12	0.00	0.00	0.00	0.00	0.00	0.00
Suburban	36.88	0.00	0.00	0.00	0.00	0.00	0.00	0.00
Buffalo								
Central City	12.28	18.25	39.22	3.30	1.58	11.40	0.00	0.87
Suburban	5.56	0.00	0.00	0.00	0.95	6.38	0.00	0.21
New York City								
Central City	5.04	12.05	0.00	4.67	1.23	2.40	15.60	4.19
Suburban	19.61	11.95	2.41	0.25	0.22	13.57	5.99	0.74
Rochester								
Central City	18.52	0.00	0.00	0.00	0.00	30.20	18.94	0.76
Suburban	0.00	29.95	0.00	0.00	0.00	1.62	0.00	0.00
Syracuse								
Central City	10.03	0.00	0.00	6.78	1.06	4.91	41.39	0.00
Suburban	6.69	21.73	0.00	0.00	1.32	6.09	0.00	0.00

Utica-Rome								
Central City	42.21	0.00	0.00	0.00	0.00	34.66	0.00	0.00
Suburban	8.26	0.00	0.00	0.00	0.00	14.35	0.00	0.49
NORTH CAROLINA								
Charlotte								
Central City	39.80	20.15	0.00	0.00	2.57	8.88	0.00	0.00
Suburban	10.17	0.00	0.00	0.00	8.11	10.31	0.00	0.00
Greensboro–Winston-Salem–High Point								
Central City	4.14	51.55	0.00	1.23	0.00	33.69	0.00	1.66
Suburban	7.49	0.00	0.00	0.00	0.22	0.00	0.00	0.00
OHIO								
Akron								
Central City	0.00	45.43	0.00	0.00	0.00	0.00	0.00	0.00
Suburban	0.00	0.00	51.64	0.00	0.00	2.93	0.00	0.00
Canton								
Central City	44.66	0.00	0.00	0.00	0.00	32.87	0.00	0.00
Suburban	0.00	0.00	0.00	0.00	0.00	22.48	0.00	0.00
Cincinnati (Ky., Ind.)								
Central City	0.00	0.00	74.24	0.00	0.00	15.90	0.00	3.09
Suburban	4.67	0.00	0.00	0.00	0.00	7.16	0.00	0.09
Cleveland								
Central City	28.98	25.33	0.00	0.00	0.00	10.85	16.65	4.17
Suburban	6.37	0.00	0.00	0.00	0.00	6.88	0.00	0.74
Columbus								
Central City	2.51	0.00	76.87	0.00	0.00	4.94	0.00	8.30
Suburban	0.00	0.00	0.00	0.00	0.00	6.64	0.00	0.74

	Enrollment in public colleges and universities				Enrollment in private colleges and universities			
	Two-year colleges	Comprehensive colleges & universities	Doctoral-granting institutions	Professional & specialized institutions	Two-year colleges	Liberal arts colleges	Doctoral-granting institutions	Professional & specialized institutions
OHIO cont.:								
Dayton								
Central City	10.53%	29.24%	0.00%	0.00%	1.82%	34.88%	0.00%	1.26%
Suburban	2.01	7.20	0.00	0.00	0.69	12.34	0.00	0.00
Toledo (Mich.)								
Central City	0.00	44.34	0.00	0.19	0.83	1.92	0.00	0.00
Suburban	8.09	44.31	0.00	0.00	0.28	0.00	0.00	0.00
Youngstown-Warren								
Central City	0.00	93.68	0.00	0.00	0.00	0.00	0.00	0.00
Suburban	6.32	0.00	0.00	0.00	0.00	0.00	0.00	0.00
OKLAHOMA								
Oklahoma City								
Central City	3.27	0.00	0.00	2.77	2.51	7.64	0.00	0.00
Suburban	1.06	26.57	51.87	0.00	0.00	4.31	0.00	0.00
Tulsa								
Central City	0.00	0.00	0.00	0.00	7.78	12.66	79.55	0.00
Suburban	0.00	0.00	0.00	0.00	0.00	0.00	0.00	0.00
OREGON								
Portland (Wash.)								
Central City	26.86	23.48	0.00	2.83	0.76	12.50	0.00	2.06
Suburban	27.54	0.00	0.00	0.00	0.00	3.92	0.00	0.00

PENNSYLVANIA

Allentown-Bethlehem-Easton (N.J.)								
Central City	29.46	0.00	0.00	0.00	0.00	35.36	27.81	0.67
Suburban	0.00	0.00	0.00	0.00	0.00	6.84	0.00	0.26
Harrisburg								
Central City	28.54	0.00	0.00	0.00	0.00	0.00	0.00	0.00
Suburban	0.00	49.47	0.00	1.95	0.00	17.30	0.00	2.75
Lancaster								
Central City	0.00	0.00	0.00	0.00	1.92	27.44	0.00	1.03
Suburban	0.00	52.84	0.00	0.00	0.00	16.74	0.00	0.00
Philadelphia								
Central City	2.84	1.16	15.93	0.00	0.98	12.46	9.87	6.19
Suburban	9.80	10.22	18.01	0.20	0.82	12.64	0.00	0.96
Pittsburgh								
Central City	8.49	0.00	36.47	0.00	0.00	5.80	17.11	6.11
Suburban	10.69	10.49	0.00	0.00	0.00	4.82	0.00	0.00
Wilkes-Barre-Hazleton								
Central City	28.31	0.00	0.00	0.00	0.00	61.91	0.00	0.00
Suburban	0.00	0.00	0.00	0.00	0.00	9.78	0.00	0.00

RHODE ISLAND

Providence-Pawtucket-Warwick (Mass.)								
Central City	7.77	13.93	0.00	0.00	0.00	14.26	12.45	12.22
Suburban	0.00	0.00	32.72	0.00	2.05	4.55	0.00	0.00

	Enrollment in public colleges and universities				Enrollment in private colleges and universities			
	Two-year colleges	Comprehensive colleges & universities	Doctoral-granting institutions	Professional & specialized institutions	Two-year colleges	Liberal arts colleges	Doctoral-granting institutions	Professional & specialized institutions
SOUTH CAROLINA								
Charleston								
Central City	18.96%	30.74%	0.00%	11.46%	7.51%	31.33%	0.00%	0.00%
Suburban	0.00	0.00	0.00	0.00	0.00	0.00	0.00	0.00
Columbia								
Central City	4.73	0.00	74.04	0.00	3.18	14.26	0.00	0.99
Suburban	0.00	0.00	0.00	0.00	0.00	0.00	0.00	0.00
Greenville								
Central City	10.27	0.00	0.00	0.00	0.00	37.17	0.00	0.00
Suburban	0.00	0.00	47.28	0.00	3.40	1.86	0.00	0.00
TENNESSEE								
Chattanooga (Ga.)								
Central City	13.98	52.33	0.00	0.00	0.00	17.91	0.00	0.00
Suburban	0.00	0.00	0.00	0.00	0.00	15.78	0.00	0.00
Knoxville								
Central City	0.00	0.00	92.68	0.00	0.00	4.32	0.00	0.81
Suburban	0.00	0.00	0.00	0.00	0.00	2.55	0.00	0.00
Memphis (Ark.)								
Central City	5.20	58.44	0.00	5.41	0.00	9.14	19.91	1.90
Suburban	0.00	0.00	0.00	0.00	0.00	0.00	0.00	0.00

Nashville								
Central City	2.77	32.01	0.00	0.00	2.39	52.37	0.00	7.83
Suburban	0.00	0.00	0.00	0.00	2.62	0.00	0.00	0.00
TEXAS								
Beaumont–Port Arthur–Orange								
Central City	0.00	100.00	0.00	0.00	0.00	0.00	0.00	0.00
Suburban	0.00	0.00	0.00	0.00	0.00	0.00	0.00	0.00
Dallas								
Central City	24.04	0.00	0.00	1.07	0.00	6.02	19.85	1.91
Suburban	0.00	0.00	40.50	1.58	1.08	2.66	0.00	1.24
El Paso								
Central City	0.00	100.00	0.00	0.00	0.00	0.00	0.00	0.00
Suburban	0.00	0.00	0.00	0.00	0.00	0.00	0.00	0.00
Fort Worth								
Central City	17.22	0.00	0.00	0.00	0.29	4.98	18.20	5.22
Suburban	12.93	39.95	0.00	0.00	0.00	1.17	0.00	0.00
Houston								
Central City	0.00	8.58	40.05	1.16	6.84	4.34	4.88	1.72
Suburban	24.47	7.16	0.00	0.00	0.00	0.00	0.00	0.00
San Antonio								
Central City	64.04	0.00	0.00	1.22	0.00	39.24	0.00	0.20
Suburban	0.00	0.00	0.00	0.00	0.00	3.76	0.00	0.00
UTAH								
Salt Lake City								
Central City	6.40	0.00	83.84	0.00	6.51	3.21	0.00	0.00
Suburban	0.00	0.00	0.00	0.00	0.00	0.00	0.00	0.00

	Enrollment in public colleges and universities				Enrollment in private colleges and universities			
	Two-year colleges	Comprehensive colleges & universities	Doctoral-granting institutions	Professional & specialized institutions	Two-year colleges	Liberal arts colleges	Doctoral-granting institutions	Professional & specialized institutions
VIRGINIA								
Norfolk-Portsmouth								
Central City	14.71	80.24	0.00	0.00	0.00	5.04	0.00	0.00
Suburban	0.00	0.00	0.00	0.00	0.00	0.00	0.00	0.00
Richmond								
Central City	0.00	61.56	0.00	0.00	0.00	26.44	0.00	0.51
Suburban	8.02	0.00	0.00	0.00	0.00	3.47	0.00	0.00
WASHINGTON								
Seattle-Everett								
Central City	27.90	0.00	45.33	0.00	0.00	7.35	0.00	0.00
Suburban	18.60	0.00	0.00	0.00	0.00	0.67	0.00	0.12
Tacoma								
Central City	46.08	0.00	0.00	0.00	0.00	53.92	0.00	0.00
Suburban	0.00	0.00	0.00	0.00	0.00	0.00	0.00	0.00
WISCONSIN								
Milwaukee								
Central City	29.65	0.00	37.60	0.00	0.52	4.35	19.28	6.09
Suburban	0.00	0.00	0.00	0.00	0.00	2.25	0.00	0.45

SOURCE: Prepared by Carnegie Commission staff from the data in U.S. Office of Education: *Opening Fall Enrollment in Higher Education, 1970, Supplementary Information, Institutional Data,* Washington, D.C., 1971.

Appendix D: Percentage of Different Populations within Commuting Distance of a Free-Access College in each Metropolitan Area of 1 Million or More

Metropolitan area	Population in millions	Percent within commuting distance			
		White	Black	Mexican American	Total
Anaheim	0.70	89	—*	89	89
City	0.29	100	—	100	100
Fringe	0.42	81	—	81	81
Atlanta	1.02	29	9	—	25
City	0.49	18	4	—	13
Fringe	0.53	36	28	—	34
Baltimore	1.73	38	36	—	37
City	0.94	36	38	—	37
Fringe	0.79	39	25	—	38
Boston	2.60	30	2	—*	21
City	0.70	16	0	—	15
Fringe	1.90	35	16	—	35
Buffalo	1.31	33	10	—	32
City	0.53	19	2	—	17
Fringe	0.77	42	60	—	42
Chicago	6.22	57	63	58	58
City	3.56	69	63	58^2	67
Fringe	2.67	45	61	—	46
Cincinnati	1.27	5	1	—	5
City	0.50	0	0	—	0
Fringe	0.77	11	8	—	10
Cleveland	1.91	21	42	—	24
City	0.88	24	43	—	30
Fringe	1.03	22	—	—	19

Metropolitan area	Population in millions	Percent within commuting distance			
		White	Black	Mexican American	Total
Dallas	1.12	10	34	32	14
City	0.68	11	41	39	18
Fringe	0.44	8	7	—	7
Denver	0.93	34	50	42	35
City	0.49	46	51	54	47
Fringe	0.44	22	—	13	22
Detroit	3.76	29	24	—	29
City	1.67	13	22	—	16
Fringe	2.09	39	42	—	39
Houston	1.42	18	23	11	18
City	0.94	10	27	5	13
Fringe	0.48	31	9	24	28
Kansas City	1.09	17	52	—	21
City	0.60	35	54	—	38
Fringe	0.50	0	—	—	0
Los Angeles	6.04	59	38	71	58
City	2.82	45	26	51	44
Fringe	3.22	69	74	88	71
Miami	0.94	43	95	—	50
City	0.29	95	90	—	94
Fringe	0.64	28	52	—	31
Milwaukee	1.28	19	92	—	23
City	0.74	32	93	—	37
Fringe	0.54	2	—	—	2
Minneapolis	1.48	25	26	—	25
City	0.80	26	27	—	26
Fringe	0.69	24	—	—	24
Newark	1.69	27	71	—	33
City	0.41	68	94	—	77
Fringe	1.28	14	35	—	20
New Orleans	0.91	31	34	—	32
City	0.63	43	40	—	42
Fringe	0.28	12	4	—	10
New York	10.69	30	21	36	29
City	7.78	30	20	36	29
Fringe	2.91	29	27	31	29

Metropolitan area	Population in millions	Percent within commuting distance			
		White	Black	Mexican American	Total
Paterson	1.19	0	0	—	0
City	0.28	0	0	—	0
Fringe	0.91	0	0	—	0
Philadelphia	4.34	26	43	—	29
City	2.00	23	46	—	29
Fringe	2.34	29	32	—	29
Pittsburgh	2.41	27	46	—	28
City	0.60	33	46	—	35
Fringe	1.80	25	45	—	26
St. Louis	2.10	43	60	—	46
City	0.75	68	78	—	71
Fringe	1.35	33	12	—	32
San Bernardino	0.81	43	61	49	45
City	0.22	73	95	99	77
Fringe	0.59	32	36	34	32
San Diego	1.03	38	49	46	39
City	0.57	28	50	42	31
Fringe	0.46	49	—	51	49
San Francisco	2.65	55	55	64	55
City	1.11	36	44	39	37
Fringe	1.54	68	80	63	68
Seattle	1.11	44	54	—	45
City	0.56	31	56	—	32
Fringe	0.55	57	—	—	57
Washington, D.C.	2.08	70	75	—	71
City	0.76	82	81	—	82
Fringe	1.31	67	45	—	65
All major SMSA†	65.81	36	41	50	37
City	32.58	36	42	42	37
Fringe	33.23	37	37	68	37

*Dash (—) = base too small for reliable estimate.
† Standard Metropolitan Statistical Areas.
SOURCE: Warren W. Willingham, *Free-Access Higher Education,* College Entrance Examination Board, 1970, pp. 196–198.

Appendix E: Estimated Needs for New Comprehensive Colleges and Community Colleges or New Campuses of Existing Institutions in Large Metropolitan Areas

	Estimated needs for new colleges, 1980	
	Comprehensive colleges	Community colleges
New England states		
Connecticut		
Bridgeport	1	
Hartford	1	1*
New Haven	1	
Massachusetts		
Boston		2–3
Springfield (Conn.)		1
Worcester		1–2
Rhode Island		
Providence		1–2
North Atlantic states		
District of Columbia		
Washington (Md., and Va.)		3–5‡
Maryland		
Baltimore		1–2
New Jersey		
Jersey City	1	2–3
Newark	1	2–3
Paterson–Clifton Passaic	1–2	2
New York		
Albany-Schenectady-Troy	1	1
Buffalo		1

	Estimated needs for new colleges, 1980	
	Comprehensive colleges	Community colleges
New York City	3–4	4–5
Rochester		1–2
Syracuse	1	1
Pennsylvania		
Allentown-Bethlehem-Easton (N.J.)	1	
Philadelphia	2–3	2–3
Pittsburgh	1–2	1
North Midwest states		
Illinois		
Chicago	2–3	3–4
Indiana		
Gary–Hammond–East Chicago	1	1*
Indianapolis	2	1–2
Michigan		
Detroit	1–2	2–3
Grand Rapids	1	1–2
Ohio		
Akron		1–2
Cincinnati (Ky.-Ind.)	2	1–2
Cleveland	1	1–2
Columbus	1	1
Dayton	1	1
Toledo (Mich.)	1	1–2
Youngstown-Warren	1	1
Wisconsin		
Milwaukee	1–2	1–2
Central states		
Minnesota		
Minneapolis–St. Paul	1–2	
Missouri		
Kansas City (Kans.)	1*	1
St. Louis (Ill.)	1–2	1–2

	Estimated needs for new colleges, 1980	
	Comprehensive colleges	Community colleges
Nebraska		
Omaha (Iowa)		1
Southeast states		
Alabama		
Birmingham		1
Florida		
Fort Lauderdale–Hollywood	1	1–2
Jacksonville	1§	1–2
Miami	1§	2–3
Tampa–St. Petersburg	1	1–2
Georgia		
Atlanta	1	1–2
Kentucky		
Louisville (Ind.)	1	1–2
Louisiana		
New Orleans	1	1–2
North Carolina		
Greensboro–Winston-Salem–High Point		1**
Tennessee		
Memphis (Ark.)	1	1–2
Nashville		1
Virginia		
Norfolk-Portsmouth		1–2
Richmond		1–2
Southwest states		
Arizona		
Phoenix	1	1–2
Oklahoma		
Oklahoma City	1	1
Texas		
Dallas	1	1
Fort Worth		1–2

	Estimated needs for new colleges, 1980	
	Comprehensive colleges	Community colleges
Houston	1	2–3
San Antonio	1	1
Mountain states		
Colorado		
Denver		1–2
Utah		
Salt Lake City	1	1
Pacific states		
California		
Anaheim–Santa Ana– Garden Grove	1	2–3
Los Angeles–Long Beach	2–3	2–4
Sacramento	1	1–2
San Bernardino	1	2–3
San Diego	1	1–2
San Francisco–Oakland	1–2	2–4
San Jose	1	2–3
Hawaii		
Honolulu	1	1**
Oregon Portland (Wash.)	1	1–2
Washington		
Seattle-Everett	1	1–2
Total needs for new colleges in large metropolitan areas	57–68	80–126

* NOTE: Carnegie Commission on Higher Education, *New Students and New Places,* McGraw-Hill Book Company, New York, N.Y., 1971, Table 11, pp. 143–151.

‡ Additional colleges are needed chiefly in the suburbs.

§ A new university that could serve as a comprehensive college has been established.

** Not in original estimates in *New Students and New Places* — added in this report.

Part B: Institutions Needed for Metropolitan Areas less than 500,000 Population*

Additional Comprehensive Colleges

Canton, Ohio

Davenport–Rock Island–Moline, Iowa

Flint, Michigan

Oxnard-Ventura, California

Peoria, Illinois

Tacoma, Washington

Tulsa, Oklahoma

Utica-Rome, New York

Wilmington, Delaware

Additional Community Colleges

Beaumont–Port Arthur–Orange, Texas

Binghamton, New York

Canton, Ohio

Charleston, South Carolina

Chattanooga, Tennessee

Columbia, South Carolina

El Paso, Texas

Flint, Michigan

Greenville, South Carolina

Harrisburg, Pennsylvania

Knoxville, Tennessee

Lancaster, Pennsylvania

Little Rock–North Little Rock, Arkansas

Mobile, Alabama

Orlando, Florida

Tulsa, Oklahoma

Wichita, Kansas

Wilkes-Barre–Hazleton, Pennsylvania

* Original estimates for new institutions in metropolitan areas were limited to areas with populations in excess of 500,000. The following are additional urban needs for areas with populations between 100,000 and 500,000.

Appendix F: Survey of College Community Relations and Urban and Minority Affairs as Reported by a Member of the Administration

In 1969, Dr. George Nash conducted a study entitled *University and the City* and sponsored by the Twentieth Century Fund. As a part of that study, he mailed questionnaires to all universities in the nation and to all four-year accredited colleges in or near cities of 100,000 or more (approximately 600). He received 384 usable responses.

The questionnaire included a list of 20 activities that colleges or universities might have undertaken to help alleviate the urban crisis. Dr. Nash's correlational analysis of the 20 items revealed that the one item most highly associated with the others was the presence or absence of an urban administrator. Those institutions that had appointed administrators specifically to deal with the urban crisis were likely to score positively on 14 of the 19 other items. The next most important factor related to a high score on urban involvement was the presence of an urban center. Also important was the goal of increasing the number of black faculty and administrators. The fourth most important component of university involvement was having prepared an inventory of what the college was already doing. Thus, those colleges that scored highest on their involvement with the urban crisis were most likely to have appointed administrators to deal with urban, community, and minority-group problems; to have an urban center; to have adopted as a goal the idea of increasing the number of black faculty and administrators; and to have compiled an inventory of what the institution was already doing.

Dr. Nash found that certain institutional characteristics were also related to a high level of involvement. Size was a major determinant of urban involvement. The average large institution scored 14 out of a possible 20, while the average small institution scored only 9. Similarly, public institutions were more likely to score high than were private. The average public institution scored 13; the average private institution scored 11.

The questionnaire used by Dr. Nash is reproduced in the following pages together with the percentage of institutions indicating each response.

*Percentage of insti-
tuitions giving
response indicated*

1. How large is the city in which your institution is located? (If your institution has more than one campus, please reply only for the main campus.)

    1. ( ) Large (over 500,000 or the suburb of a large city) _____ 41

    2. ( ) Medium (50,000 to 500,000 or the suburb of a medium size city _____ 40

    3. ( ) Small (less than 50,000) _____ 19

2. *(a)* How would you characterize the location of the campus (or principal campus) of your institution?

    1. ( ) In the inner city, the downtown area or adjacent to it _____ 19

    2. ( ) In the city, but not in the main downtown area _____ 45

    3. ( ) In a suburb _____ 27

    4. ( ) In a non-urban area, other than above _____ 9

(b) IF THE ANSWER TO 2a IS OTHER THAN 1: Does your institution have any buildings or another (subsidiary) campus in a downtown or inner city area?

    1. ( ) Yes: please specify _____ 18

    2. ( ) No _____ 82

3. *(a)** Has your institution prepared an inventory of what it is doing in the way of urban, community and minority affairs?

    1. ( ) Yes we have compiled a fairly comprehensive inventory of what we are doing _____

    2. ( ) We have compiled a list of some of the things we are doing, but it is not comprehensive _____

    3. ( ) We have collected a comprehensive inventory of what we are doing, but have not yet written it up _____   47

    4. ( ) We have compiled an inventory of some of the things we are doing, but have not yet written it up _____

    5. ( ) We are planning to or thinking of preparing such an inventory _____ 53

6. ( ) We have no plans at present to conduct such an inventory ⸻ 53

(b) If your institution has prepared such an inventory please print the title and date here and mail us a copy.

⸻

4.* Does your institution have one (or more) administrator(s) in urban, community, and/or minority affairs who spends (or spend) at least half his time in these activities?

  1. ( ) Yes: Please print his (their) name(s) and title(s) ⸻ 47

⸻

⸻

  2. ( ) No, but we are planning to appoint such a person ⸻ }
  3. ( ) No ⸻ } 53

5. *(a)** Does your institution have a center or a research bureau either active or principally involved in the areas of urban or community or minority affairs?

  1. ( ) Yes ⸻ 37
  2. ( ) No, but we are planning to ⸻ }
  3. ( ) No ⸻ } 63

*(b)** IF YES: In what areas is (are) the centers(s) involved? (Check all that apply.)

  1. ( ) Education graduate ⸻ 41
  2. ( ) Education undergraduate ⸻ 50
  3. ( ) Community service ⸻ 76
  4. ( ) Research ⸻ 68

6. Does your institution have a long range educational plan?

  1. ( ) Yes ⸻ 73
  2. ( ) No, but we are planning to ⸻ 23
  3. ( ) No ⸻ 4

7. Does your institution have either a master campus (physical) plan or a planner?

  1. ( ) Yes, both ⸻ 60
  2. ( ) Plan, but no planner ⸻ 27
  3. ( ) Planner, but no plan ⸻ 5
  4. ( ) Neither ⸻ 8

8. Has your institution obtained property for expansion under Federal urban renewal legislation?

1. ( ) Yes _____	12
2. ( ) No, but we plan to _____	6
3. ( ) No, but we would like to _____	10
4. ( ) No _____	73

9. Does your institution have a parking problem either on or nearby the campus?

1. ( ) Yes, but it is in fairly good control because of our rules _____	54
2. ( ) Yes and it is not in good control _____	23
3. ( ) No _____	23

10. Has your institution constructed or aided in the construction of any of the following types of parking facilities? (Check all that apply.)

1. ( ) Parking garage on campus _____	10
2. ( ) Parking lot on campus _____	98
3. ( ) Parking garage off campus _____	1
4. ( ) Parking lot off campus _____	8

11. Does your institution have a need to expand the size of its present campus?

1. ( ) Yes _____	51
2. ( ) No _____	19
3. ( ) No, and we are OK for the foreseeable future _____	30

12.* Has your institution engaged in any activities to improve physically the neighborhood or the community adjacent to the campus?

1. ( ) Yes _____	36
2. ( ) No, but we are planning to _____	
3. ( ) No _____	64

13. Approximately what percent of the full-time undergraduates at your institution live in the following types of housing?

_____ on campus or contiguous to the campus in housing owned by the institution _____	43
_____ in fraternity or sorority houses _____	4
_____ off campus but separate from parents _____	16
_____ with parents or family _____	37

14. *(a)* Does your institution provide assistance for housing the faculty?

1. ( ) Yes _____	49
2. ( ) No _____	51

(b) IF YES: Which of the following forms of assistance do you
provide? (Check all that apply.)

1. ( ) Institutionally owned housing _____	67
2. ( ) Loans for purchase or renovation of housing _____	23
3. ( ) A directory of housing available _____	56

(c) IF YOUR INSTITUTION PROVIDES INSTITUTIONALLY
OWNED HOUSING FOR FACULTY: About what percent of
the full-time faculty live in such housing?

1. ( ) 70% or more _____	6
2. ( ) 40–69% _____	9
3. ( ) 20–39% _____	13
4. ( ) Less than 20% _____	72
5. ( ) Don't know _____	0

15. What percent of your full-time faculty (who teach on the main
campus) do you estimate live within two miles of the main campus?

1. ( ) 70% or more _____	21
2. ( ) 40–69% _____	23
3. ( ) 20–39% _____	24
4. ( ) Less than 20% _____	32
5. ( ) Don't know _____	0

16. What services does the institution get free on campus from some
governmental agency?

(a) Fire Protection

We pay nothing _____	72
We pay something or exchange goods or services _____	20
We get no such service. We provide our own _____	8

(b) Refuse or trash removal

We pay nothing _____	10
We pay something or exchange goods or services _____	25
We get no such service. We provide our own _____	65

(c) Water or sewage

We pay nothing _____	13
We pay something or exchange goods or services _____	70
We get no such service. We provide our own _____	17

17. *(a)* Does your institution have campus police?

1. ( ) Yes _____	82
2. ( ) No _____	18

(b) IF YES: How many men are regularly employed during the academic year? ____13____

(c) IF YES: What is the approximate yearly budget? _$99,400_

18. *(a)* Does your institution contribute either directly or indirectly toward police protection of the area surrounding the campus?

    1. ( ) Yes _____ 17

    2. ( ) No _____ 83

(b) IF YES: About how much does your institution contribute per year? ____$30,000____

19. Is there a crime or safety problem for your students, staff or property either on campus or in the surrounding area?

    1. ( ) Yes, in both areas _____ 34

    2. ( ) Yes, off campus, but not on _____ 7

    3. ( ) Yes, on campus, but not off _____ 4

    4. ( ) Neither _____ 55

20. *(a)** Does the institution have an organized program of higher education for disadvantaged students whose cultural, economic and educational handicaps (in comparison with your regular student body) classify them as "high-risk" enrollees?

    1. ( ) Yes _____⎫

    2. ( ) No, but we are planning one _____⎬ 79

    3. ( ) No _____⎭ 21

Please write the name and title of person in charge of the program

_____

(b)* IF YES: Does the program include? (Check all that apply.)

    1. ( ) Recruiting _____ 92

    2. ( ) Lower admissions requirements _____ 68

    3. ( ) Extra counseling and guidance _____ 95

    4. ( ) Financial aid _____ 95

    5. ( ) Specially designed courses _____ 43

    6. ( ) Extra help (tutoring, smaller classes, lighter academic load, etc.) _____ 89

    7. ( ) Other compensations. Please specify: _____ 10

(c) IF YES: What year was the program started? ___1967___

(d) IF YES: Approximately how many students are now involved? ____89____

21. What is the approximate full-time undergraduate enrollment of

students of various ethnic backgrounds? [If there are none of a group,
enter zero (0).]

    ( ) We don't have this information

    a. Black (Negro, Afro-American, African) _____160_____

    b. Spanish surnamed American _____70_____

    c. American Indian _____29_____

    d. Total full-time undergraduate enrollment in the fall of
this academic year _____4,935_____

22. *(a)** Are you presently seeking to expand the proportion of
minority group students enrolled at your institution?

    1. ( ) Yes ——————————————————— 84

    2. ( ) No ——————————————————— 16

    (b)* IF YES: What type of minority group students are you try-
ing to attract? Please circle the letter from Question 21 above:

    a. ——————————————————— 97

    b. ——————————————————— 48

    c. ——————————————————— 32

    d. ———————————————————

23.* Does your institution participate in the Federally funded Upward Bound Program to help poor or minority group students prepare
for college?

    1. ( ) Yes ———————————————

    2. ( ) No, but we would like to or have applied and weren't ⎫ 64

    funded ——————————————— ⎭

    3. ( ) No ——————————————————— 36

24.* Does your institution have any program to regularly bring
urban, poor, or minority group students on campus during the
academic year?

    1. ( ) No ——————————————————— 49

    2. ( ) Yes, please describe it briefly ——————— 51

25.* Do children from the community use campus facilities for
recreation or entertainment?

    1. ( ) Yes, frequently ——————————————— 40

    2. ( ) Yes, but infrequently ————————— ⎫ 60

    3. ( ) No ——————————————————— ⎭

26.* Do community groups or organizations not related to the college use the facilities of your institution?

    1. ( ) Yes, frequently —————————————   51

    2. ( ) Yes, but infrequently —————————————⎫

    3. ( ) No ———————————————————⎬ 49

27.* Do people from the community, not enrolled in your institution, attend recreational or artistic events on campus?

    1. ( ) Yes, many do —————————————   71

    2. ( ) Yes, but only a few do —————————⎫

    3. ( ) No ————————————————————⎬ 29

28. *(a)* How many full-time faculty members are black (Negro, Afro-American or African)? __4.7__   ( ) We don't know.

    (b) How many administrators are black (Negro, Afro-American or African)? __1.4__   ( ) We don't know.

    (c) How many of your trustees are black (Negro, Afro-American or African)? __0.3__   ( ) We don't know.

29.* Is your institution actively seeking to expand the number of either full-time black faculty members or administrators?

    1. ( ) Yes, faculty and administrators ———————   66

    2. ( ) Yes faculty, not administrators ——————⎫

    3. ( ) Yes administrators, not faculty —————⎬ 34

    4. ( ) Neither ————————————————⎭

30.* Does your institution offer any non-credit courses to people from the community (similar to those offered by extension centers at some universities)?

    1. ( ) Yes, we have a large program ———————   23

    2. ( ) Yes, but our program is small ——————⎫

    3. ( ) No, but we are planning to offer such courses ——⎬ 77

    4. ( ) No ————————————————————⎭

31.* Does your institution admit part-time students for courses for credit?

    1. ( ) Yes ————————————————————   94

    2. ( ) No ————————————————————   6

32.* Is there an urban studies undergraduate major or minor in your institution?

    1. ( ) A major ————————————————⎫

    2. ( ) A minor ————————————————⎬ 15

3. ( ) Neither, but we have at least one course dealing
specifically with the city or urban problems _____

4. ( ) None of the above, but we are planning courses in
this area _____

5. ( ) None of the above _____

    85

33. *(a)** Are any of your undergraduate students involved in tutoring programs or any other similar volunteer programs in the community?
    1. ( ) Yes _____   92
    2. ( ) No _____   8

  (b) IF YES: About how many students are involved this year?
    _____ 129 _____

  (c) IF YES: Are there more students involved this academic
year than last year?
    1. ( ) More this year _____   54
    2. ( ) About the same number _____   41
    3. ( ) More last year _____   5
    4. ( ) Don't know _____

34.* Do undergraduates receive course credit for work done in
the community?
    1. ( ) Yes _____
    2. ( ) No, but we are in the process of planning such a   44
    program _____
    3. ( ) No _____   56

35. Does your institution have any sort of cooperative work-study
program where students work off campus part of the year on a
systematic basis?
    1. ( ) Yes _____   36
    2. ( ) No _____   64

36. Which of the following exist at your institution?
  *(a)** An association of black students
    1. Yes _____   71
    2. It is being planned but not yet active _____   3
    3. No _____   26

  *(b)** A center for black students
    1. Yes _____
    2. It is being planned but not yet active _____   21
    3. No _____   79

*Percentage of insti-
tuitions giving
response indicated*

*(c)** A black studies program
    1. Yes ————————————————⎫
    2. It is being planned but not yet active ———————⎬   42
    3. No ———————————————————   58

*(d)** (IF NO PROGRAM) At least one course in black history,
literature, identity or a similar subject
    1. Yes ————————————————————   66
    2. It is being planned but not yet active ———————   12
    3. No —————————————————————   22

*(e)** Chapters of black fraternities or sororities
    1. Yes ————————————————————   20
    2. It is being planned but not yet active ———————   3
    3. No —————————————————————   77

37. *(a)* Have the students at your institution staged any sort of
protest within the last two academic years?
    1. ( ) Yes, we had a major protest ———————————   15
    2. ( ) Yes, but it was minor —————————————   53
    3. ( ) No ————————————————————   33

(b) IF YES: What was this protest related to? (Check all that
apply)
    1. ( ) Any area related to urban and minority affairs ———   42
    2. ( ) Related to the war —————————————   34
    3. ( ) Something else ————————————————   60

38. *(a)* What proportion of your non-academic employees presently
belong to unions?
    1. ( ) Most ———————————————————   8
    2. ( ) Some, but not most —————————————   19
    3. ( ) Few ————————————————————   24
    4. ( ) None ————————————————————   50

(b) IF ANY UNIONIZED: Which types are? (Check all that are.)
    1. ( ) Clerical ————————————————————   13
    2. ( ) Technical (lab, medical, other research, etc.) ———   7
    3. ( ) Skilled workers (such as electricians or carpenters) —   66
    4. ( ) Maintenance workers —————————————   74
    5. ( ) Kitchen workers —————————————————   34

39.* Does your institution have a program for upgrading lower level
non-academic employees?
    1. ( ) Yes —————————————————————⎫
    2. ( ) No, but we are planning one ———————————⎬   57
    3. ( ) No —————————————————————   43

40. IF A PRIVATE INSTITUTION WITH AN ENDOWMENT:
Does your institution have a program whereby its endowment funds
are either invested in things the institution approves of or withheld
from things the institution disapproves of or considers unethical?

1. ( ) Yes _____	35
2. ( ) No, but we are planning to switch our investments __	1
3. ( ) No _____	55

41. How would you characterize relations between the college and
the community immediately surrounding it?

1. ( ) Good _____	72
2. ( ) Fair _____	27
3. ( ) Poor _____	1

Sixteen predominantly black colleges excluded from the total shown on this question.

General information on institutions responding		
Percentage of black students enrolled		3.3%
Full-time undergrad enrollment		4,441
Predominantly Negro college		
No		95
Yes		5
College type		
Public university		25
Private university		12
Public college		11
Private college		47
Black college		5
Control		
Public		37
Private		63
Sex composition		
Coed		73
Coord		3
Men		8
Women		16
Size		
Small		25

General information institutions responding (cont.)		
Size (cont.)		
Medium		45
Large		30
Urban type		
Inner city		11
Other city		47
Suburb		21
Rural		21

Appendix G: Survey of Cities in 31 Major Metropolitan Areas

In an effort to obtain information about the organization of higher education resources within metropolitan areas and the relation of city governments to universities and colleges in major cities, brief questionnaires were sent in March 1971 to the mayors or city managers of 38 cities located in the 31 standard statistical metropolitan areas with populations in excess of 1 million. A similar questionnaire was sent to the agency assigned responsibility for coordinating higher education in each of the 19 states in which these 31 areas were located. Responses were received from 14 states in which 24 of the major metropolitan areas were located and from 25 cities located in 23 major metropolitan areas. Information obtained from these responses is summarized below.

Metropolitan coordinating agencies
Seventeen of the mayor/city managers responded that there were no higher education coordinating agencies in their city, and eight indicated that there were. In at least two instances, a no response was given although a voluntary higher education coordinating agency has existed in the area for some time. In the cases of some of the yes responses, the agency identified as the coordinating agency is not the type usually considered as functioning in this capacity (one city named the urban observatory as the coordinating agency and another named the civil service commission). Two cities named agencies which have only very informal contacts with higher education institutions other than two-year colleges. Of the remaining four cities responding in the affirmative, it is known that at least one of the coordinating agencies is not now functioning because of lack of funds. Two of the cities which did not have coordinating agencies at the time of the survey now have such agencies.

An examination of the state responses to the same question revealed some discrepancies. In the instance in which the city had viewed the urban observatory as a coordinating agency, the state did not; another state, however, did view the urban observatory in one of its metropolitan areas as a coordinating agency. In the two metropolitan areas where coordinating agencies did exist although the cities had responded in the negative, the state agencies responded in the affirmative. State agencies were more likely to view consortia as coordinating agencies than were city respondents. (Three consortia were so identified for metropolitan areas by state agencies but were not so identified by cities.) In two cases, states named a state coordinating agency as functioning for the metropolitan area. Two additional metropolitan coordinating agencies were identified in state questionnaires for two cities which had not responded.

Only four of the metropolitan agencies identified have a formal relation to the state coordinating agencies in which they are located, and it is only these four which might be considered as operating on a level other than purely voluntary.

City liaison with higher education

Mayors and city managers were asked the following question:

Is there anyone on your staff who has special responsibility for staff work on higher education and relations with colleges and universities?

Fifteen of the cities responded yes. But in four of these cities the person given the responsibility carried the title Personnel Director or Training Officer, and it is assumed that the liaison may be limited primarily to the professional training needs of the city employees.

Inventories and projections of higher education needs for the metropolitan area

In response to the question:

Do you know of any inventory of higher education resources and projections of needs of student spaces in the metropolitan area?

Twenty city questionnaires contained negative responses. For three of these areas, state questionnaires indicated that such inventories and projections were available.

City funds for higher education

Although local tax funds provide support for many public two-year colleges, in most cities these funds do not go through the city budget but are collected and dispersed separately through an independent legal entity established for the purpose of governing the community college district. Only five of the cities responded that there were any allocations for operating or capital expenditures for institutions of higher education in their city budgets. Of those responding, New York City makes by far the heaviest contribution to higher education through its city budget, and Philadelphia and Washington, D.C., also make substantial contributions. Atlanta and Minneapolis have some funds allocated to higher education through their city budgets, and in the city of Cincinnati two mills of every assessed property tax dollar collected by the city are allocated to the University of Cincinnati.

Public service activities

Respondents for the questionnaires to cities were asked to identify those public-service activities of colleges and universities in their metropolitan areas which they considered to be particularly valuable. Eight of the respondents did not answer this question. Two others referred the Commission to other agencies within the city or to the universities and colleges for the response. The most frequently identified valuable public service furnished by colleges and universities was professional training programs for city employees. Each of the following received three mentions:

Consultation with city staff on city projects such as model cities

Special research projects

Student intern programs in city government units

Minority education or outreach programs

Each of the following received one mention:

Urban observatory programs

Drug education programs

Collaboration with youth programs

Civil defense and emergency preparedness programs

Prison project

Land-grant activities

Cities were also asked to identify any additional public service activities that they believe are needed and could be provided by colleges and universities in their areas. The rate of failure to respond on this question was very high with relatively few of the city respondents identifying particular services which they thought might be supplied by colleges and universities. Of those who did respond, one suggested that colleges and universities should provide money to the city government and other suggestions were as follows:

Greater contacts between university and college personnel and city officials (e.g., city sanitarian and sanitary engineering department at the university)

Law enforcement courses as a regular part of police recruiting

Executive development programs for city officials

Labor management courses and other regular college courses on a short-term basis for city employees

Research into crime

Development of manpower allocation models with particular reference to the metropolitan area

Development of alternative solid waste disposal systems

Research on waste management

Research on land use control

Establishment of a center for guidance and general information relative to colleges and universities and other postsecondary institutions including information on financial aid

Authorization for new colleges

State agencies were asked if any new colleges had been authorized for the major metropolitan areas in their states. No new colleges had been authorized for ten of the major metropolitan areas. In other metropolitan areas twelve community colleges had been authorized in seven major metropolitan areas, and three four-year public institutions had been authorized in three major metropolitan areas.

Metropolitan education counseling services

State agencies were asked to indicate whether there were any educational counseling services for residents in the metropolitan areas other than those that were available through the student's high school or individual colleges or universities. Eight states responded that there were no such services. Two states indicated that there were private (for profit) services agencies available. Other states mentioned the following agencies as providing counseling services:

State department of education

Jewish vocational service

Veterans administration

Adult education council

Model cities program

Action centers

Mobile centers and storefront centers through various federally funded programs

Higher educational aids board

Various community organizations

Appendix H: Percentage of Current Expenses of Two-Year Public Colleges from Various Sources for the Budget Year 1967-68, as Reported by State Officials

	Federal	State	Local supporting district	Local charge-back	Student fees and tuition	Other
Alabama	21	59	0	0	18	2
* Arizona	3	47	43	6	1	0
* Arkansas	10	32	31	0	25	2
* California	3	32	60	1	0	4
Colorado	2	40	31	0	15	12
Connecticut	1	79	0	0	20[a]	0
Delaware	0	100	0	0	0	0
* Florida	5	59	11	0	24	1
Georgia[b]	4	69	0	0	25	2
Hawaii	23	75	0	0	2	0
* Idaho	2	40	27	5	24	1
* Illinois	2	31	47	6	12	2
Indiana	10	13	2	0	31	44
* Iowa	12	55	17	0	14	2
* Kansas	5	17	40	21	14	3
Kentucky	2	98	0	0	0	0
* Louisiana	24	59	0	0	8	9
* Maryland	6	21	47	1	25	0
Massachusetts	4	71	0	0	25[a]	0
* Michigan	2	36	26	0	29	7
Minnesota	2	71	0	0	27	0
* Mississippi	11	39	35	2	11	2
* Missouri	5	31	37	0	17	10
* Montana	4	59	20	0	17	0
* Nebraska	0	26	35	0	33	6

	Federal	State	Local supporting district	Local charge-back	Student fees and tuition	Other
* Nevada	0	4	0	0	34	62
* New Jersey	0	50	25	0	25	0
New Mexico	11	0	33	0	51	5
* New York	2	32	38	5	21	2
* North Carolina	2	79	11	0	8	0
* North Dakota[c]	8	42	20	0	29	1
North Dakota[d]	0	67	0	0	33	0
* Ohio	2	36	25	0	30	7
* Oklahoma	0	59	4	0	32	5
* Oregon	7	48	22	0	23	0
* Pennsylvania	7	31	31	0	23	0
Rhode Island	1	63	0	0	18	18
Tennessee	15	62	0	0	13	10
* Texas	0	51	30	0	19	0
Utah	8	67	0	0	13	1
Virginia	10	79	0	0	11	0
* Washington	11	76	0	0	13	0
* Wyoming	4	31	43	0	17	5

* States in which control and support are shared with the local community.

[a] Student fees and tuition go into the state general fund from which total operating expenses are funded.

[b] Excludes one locally controlled college.

[c] For locally controlled colleges.

[d] For state-controlled colleges.

SOURCE: Arney (1969), and as included in Medsker and Tillery (1971, pp. 116, 117).

Appendix I: Bibliographies

Useful references related to the topics discussed in this report are too numerous to list in this volume. The various publications cited in the text will provide excellent references for those studying this subject, but they hardly represent a comprehensive bibliography. Fortunately, several bibliographies or listings of programs or agencies are available in this field. For your information, we have listed those below which we found particularly helpful.

Bibliographies on City-Campus Relationships

Fink, Ira Stephen, and Joan Cooke: *Campus/Community Relationships: An Annotated Bibliography,* University of California Press, Berkeley, vol. 1, April 1971.

Fink, Ira Stephen, and Joan Cooke: *Campus/Community Relationships: An Annotated Bibliography,* University of California Press, Berkeley, vol. 2, April 1972.

Nemerov, Susan, and J. G. Paltridge: *Higher Education in an Urban Society: A Bibliography,* Center for Research and Development in Higher Education, University of California, Berkeley, August 1968.

Sources Pertaining to Particular Types of City-Related University Programs

Bischoff, Henry: *Urban Studies Now,* St. Peter's College, Jersey City, N.J., February 1972.

A Directory of University Urban Research Centers, The Urban Institute, Washington, D.C., 1969.

National Service Secretariat: *List of Publications,* Washington, D.C., n.d. (Mimeographed.)

Preparing Teachers for Urban Schools: An Annotated Bibliography for Teacher Education, Mid-Continent Regional Educational Laboratory, Kansas City, Mo., 1969.

Reports of Selected University-City Programs

Missouri University Inter-campus Seminar on Urban Problem-solving Proceedings, Columbia, vol. 1 (Dec. 3–4, 1969), vol. 2 (Feb. 16–17, 1970), vol. 3 (April 15–16, 1970).

Reports from the University of Pittsburgh University-Urban Interface Program, available through ERIC Processing and Reference Facility, 4833 Rugby Avenue, Bethesda, Md., 20014.

a. **Koleda, Michael S., et al.:** *The Student Consultant Project (SCP): A Case Study of Student Involvement in Social Action,* September 1971.

b. *Phase II Interim Report (April 1970–June 1971),* September 1971.

c. **Nehnevajsa, Jiri, and Alan Coleman:** *The Pittsburgh Goals Study: A Summary,* October 1971.

d. **Coleman, M., J. V. Cunningham, Marvin Feit, N. Johnson, P. Carter, and Joseph Colangelo:** *Is Conflict Utilization Underestimated?* University Forum Background Paper, October 1971.

e. **Nehnevajsa, Jiri:** *Pittsburgh Goals: Some Issues,* October 1971.

f. **Holden, Matthew, Jr.:** *Law & Order in the Metropolitan Area,* University Forum Background Paper, November 1971.

g. **Nehnevajsa, Jiri:** *Pittsburgh Goals: Notes on the Criminal Justice System,* November 1971.

h. **Treuting, W. L., W. T. Hall, and M. L. Baizerman:** *The University and the Community in the Domain of Health,* University Forum Background Paper, December 1971.

i. **Nehnevajsa, Jiri, and Robert C. Brictson:** *Pittsburgh Goals: Some Thoughts on Health Issues,* December 1971.

j. *Phase III Progress Report 2 (October–December 1971),* January 1972.

k. **Gow, J. Steele:** *Goals and Government of the Metropolis,* University Forum Background Paper, February 1972.

l. **Nehnevajsa, Jiri:** *Pittsburgh Goals: Notes on Metropolitanism,* February 1972.

m. *Phase III Progress Report 3 (January–March 1972),* April 1972.

n. *University-Urban Interface Program Brochure,* April 1972.

o. *The Impact of the University of Pittsburgh on the Local Economy,* Educational Systems Research Group, April 1972.

p. *University Urban Interface: Issues, Methodology, Prospects,* presented at Eastern Psychological Association 43rd Annual Meeting, Boston, by R. C. Brictson and A. C. Van Dusen, April 27–29, 1972.

q. *Phase III Progress Report 4 (April–June 1972),* June 1972.

r. **Gow, J. Steele, and Leslie Salmon-Cox:** *A University and Its Community Confront Problems and Goals,* June 1972.

s. *Phase IV Progress Report 1 (July–September 1972),* September 1972.

t. *Methodological Appendix — the Impact of the University of Pittsburgh on the Local Economy,* Educational Systems Research Group, August 1972.

u. **Nehnevajsa, Jiri:** *Pittsburgh: Goals and Futures,* September 1972.

v. **Van Dusen, A. C., and R. C. Brictson:** *Research on Communiversity Relations,* prepared for the Symposium on Academic Reform of the American Psychological Association, 1972 Annual Meeting, Honolulu, Hawaii, September 2–8, 1972.

The Urban University and The Urban Community, Metrocenter Reports, Boston University, March 9–May 31, 1966.

References

American Association of State Colleges and Universities: *A Guide to Federal Funds for Urban Programs at Colleges and Universities,* produced by Office of Urban Programs in cooperation with the Office of Urban Affairs, American Council on Education, Washington, D.C., 1971.

Arney, L. H.: "A Comparison of Patterns of Financial Support with Selected Criteria in Community Junior Colleges," unpublished doctoral dissertation, University of Florida, Gainesville, 1969.

Atlanta Service-Learning Conference Report, Southern Regional Education Board, Atlanta, 1970.

Bischoff, Henry: *Urban Studies Now,* St. Peter's College, Jersey City, N.J., 1972.

Caffrey, John: "Tax and Tax-Related Arrangements Between Colleges and Universities and Local Governments," *A.C.E. Special Report,* Washington, D.C., August 12, 1969.

Caffrey, John, and Herbert H. Isaacs: *Estimating the Impact of a College or University on the Local Economy,* American Council on Education, Washington, D.C., 1941.

Canty, Donald: "Metropolity," *City,* March-April 1972, pp. 29–44.

Carnegie Commission on Higher Education: *A Chance to Learn: An Action Agenda for Equal Opportunity in Higher Education,* McGraw-Hill Book Company, New York, 1970a.

Carnegie Commission on Higher Education: *Higher Education and the Nation's Health: Policies for Medical and Dental Education,* McGraw-Hill Book Company, New York, 1970b.

Carnegie Commission on Higher Education: *Less Time, More Options: Education Beyond the High School,* McGraw-Hill Book Company, New York, 1970c.

Carnegie Commission on Higher Education: *The Open-Door Colleges: Policies for Community Colleges,* McGraw-Hill Book Company, New York, 1970d.

Carnegie Commission on Higher Education: *The Capitol and the Campus: State Responsibility for Postsecondary Education,* McGraw-Hill Book Company, New York, 1971*a.*

Carnegie Commission on Higher Education: *New Students and New Places: Policies for the Future Growth and Development of American Higher Education,* McGraw-Hill Book Company, New York, 1971*b.*

"City Taxes and Services," an Urban Observatory Report, *Nation's Cities,* August 1971.

"The Cooperative Education Program," *American Education,* vol. 7, no. 1, p. 36, January-February 1971.

Corcoran, Thomas B.: "The Future of the Community College," report prepared under USOE contract #1-7-07-0996-4253, Washington, D.C., May 1972.

Crisis at Columbia: Report of the Fact-Finding Commission Appointed to Investigate the Disturbance at Columbia University in April and May 1968, Vintage Books, New York, 1968.

Doxiadis, C. A.: "Cities in Crisis and the University," *College and University Bulletin,* vol. 47, no. 4, October 1969.

Enarson, Harold L.: "Higher Education and Community Services," in *The Campus and Racial Crisis,* American Council on Education, Washington, D.C., 1969.

Greeley, Andrew M.: "The New Urban Studies—A Word of Caution," *Educational Record,* vol. 51, pp. 232–236, Summer 1970.

Harper, William R.: "The University and Democracy," *The Trend in Higher Education,* University of Chicago Press, Chicago, 1905.

Holleb, Doris B.: *Colleges and the Urban Poor,* D. C. Heath and Company, Boston, 1972.

The Impact of the University of Pittsburgh on the Local Economy, Educational Systems Research Group, Washington, D.C., 1972.

Jacobson, Elden E.: "Urban Curricula and the Liberal Arts Colleges," *Liberal Education,* vol. 58, pp. 286–297, May 1972.

Jenkins, Martin D.: *Guidelines for Institutional Self-Study of Involvement in Urban Affairs,* American Council on Education, Washington, D.C., 1971*a.*

Jenkins, Martin D.: *The Urban Affairs Programs of Higher Education Associations: What They Are Doing and What They Can Do,* American Council on Education, Washington, D.C., 1971*b.*

Klotsche, J. Martin: "The Role of the University in an Urban Setting," *Summary of Proceedings,* the Association of Urban Universities, Jacksonville, Fla., 1960.

Klotsche, J. Martin: *The Urban University: And the Future of Our Cities,* Harper & Row Publishers, Incorporated, New York, 1966.

Kriegel, Leonard: *Working Through: A Teacher's Journey in the Urban University,* Saturday Review Press, New York, 1972.

Kristol, Irving: "What Business Is a University In?" *Liberal Education,* vol. 56, no. 2, pp. 229–237, May 1970.

Levi, Julian: "Influence of Environment on Urban Institutions," *Educational Record,* vol. 42, pp. 137–141, April 1961.

London, Herbert: "Experimental Colleges, University Without Walls: Reform or Rip-off?" *Saturday Review,* Sept. 16, 1972, pp. 62–65.

Maier, Henry W.: "An Overview of Urban Observatories," in *Urban Observatories,* Fels Institute of Local and State Government, University of Pennsylvania, Philadelphia, 1966.

Marshall, Dale Rogers: "Metropolitan Government: Views of Minorities," in Lowdon Wingo (ed.), *The Governance of Metropolitan Regions,* no. 2, *Minority Perspectives,* Resources for the Future, Washington, D.C., 1972.

Management Information Service: *College Students in Local Government: The Urban Corps Approach,* International City Managers' Association, Washington, D.C., vol. 4, no. LS-3, March 1972.

Massachusetts Board of Education: *Higher Education in the Boston Metropolitan Area: An Overview,* part 4, Board of Higher Education Series, Boston, n.d. (Mimeographed.)

Massachusetts Board of Education: *Higher Education in the Boston SMSA: A Follow-Up Study of the Potential and Realized Demands for Higher Education,* Boston, 1971. (Mimeographed.)

Medsker, Leland L., and Dale Tillery: *Breaking the Access Barriers: A Profile of Two-Year Colleges,* sponsored by the Carnegie Commission on Higher Education, McGraw-Hill Book Company, New York, 1971.

Meyerson, Martin: "Town and Gown: The Urban Community and the University Community," *AAAS Bulletin,* vol. 22, no. 6, p. 10, April 1969. Paper delivered at a meeting of the American Academy of Arts and Sciences, March 1969.

Nash, George: *The University and the City: Eight Cases of Involvement,* a report sponsored by the Carnegie Commission on Higher Education, McGraw-Hill Book Company, New York, forthcoming.

Opinion Research Corporation: "Youth Attitudes: America's Teenagers Discuss Their Plans for Further Education and Their Career Choices," vol. 28, no. 20, Public Opinion Index, New Jersey, October, 1970.

Organization for Social and Technical Innovation: *Urban Universities: Rhetoric, Reality and Conflict,* U.S. Department of Health, Education and Welfare, Washington, D.C., 1970.

Palola, E. G., and A. R. Oswald: *Urban Multi-unit Community Colleges: Adaptation for the 70's,* Center for Research and Development in Higher Education, University of California Press, Berkeley, 1972.

Parsons, Kermit C., and Georgia K. Davis: "The Urban University and its Urban Government," *Minerva,* vol. 9, no. 3, pp. 361–385, July 1971.

Peterson, Richard E.: *American College and University Enrollment Trends in 1971,* Carnegie Commission on Higher Education, Berkeley, Calif., 1972.

"The President's Message to the Congress on Urban Problems, February 22, 1968," in *Weekly Compilation of Presidential Documents,* Washington, D.C., 1968.

Report of the Commission on Isla Vista, (Martin Trow, chairman), University of California, Santa Barbara, 1970. (Mimeographed.)

Report of the President's Committee on the Future University of Massachusetts, University of Massachusetts, Boston, December 1971.

Strang, William A.: *The University and the Local Economy,* Bureau of Business Research and Service, Madison, Wisc., 1971.

Sweet, David: paper given before the 21st Annual SREB Legislative Work Conference in New Orleans, July 21, 1972. (Mimeographed.)

U.S. Bureau of the Census: "Trends in Social and Economic Conditions in Metropolitan and Non-metropolitan Areas," in *Current Population Reports,* ser. P-23, no. 33, Washington, D.C., 1970.

U.S. Office of Education, National Center for Education Statistics: "Financial Statistics of Institutions of Higher Education," *Current Funds and Revenue Expenditures 1965–66,* Washington, D.C., 1969.

The University and the City, Office of the President, Harvard University, Cambridge, Mass., 1969.

The University of Pittsburgh: *Plan for an Office of the Urban and Community Services,* Office of the Vice-Chancellor for Program Development and Public Affairs, Pittsburgh, Penn., 1969.

The University of Pittsburgh: *The Response of an Urban University to Change,* a report to the Commission on Institutions of Higher Education of the Middle States Association of Colleges and Secondary Schools, *Vol. II, Reports of the Sub-Committees,* Pittsburgh, Penn., 1971.

The University of Pittsburgh: *University-Urban Interface Program,* Office of the Secretary, Pittsburgh, Penn., 1972.

White, Leonard, et al.: *Chicago: An Experiment in Social Science Research,* University of Chicago Press, Chicago, 1929.

Willingham, Warren W.: *Free-Access Higher Education,* College Entrance Examination Board, New York, 1970.

Willingham, Warren W.: *The No. 2 Access Problem: Transfer to the Upper Division,* American Association for Higher Education, Washington, D.C., 1972.

Wood, Robert: "The New Metropolis and the New University," *Educational Record,* vol. 46, pp. 306–311, Summer 1965.

Wood, Robert: "User Agency Policies and Mechanisms for Utilizing the Resources of Institutions of Higher Education," paper presented to the Conference on Institutions of Higher Education as a Resource in the Solution of National Problems, Washington, D.C., May 1972. (Mimeographed.)

XD Newsletter, External Degree Program, Policy Institute, Syracuse University Research Council, vol. 1, no. 2, August 1971.

Carnegie Commission on Higher Education

Sponsored Research Studies

THE NEW DEPRESSION IN HIGHER
EDUCATION:
A STUDY OF FINANCIAL CONDITIONS AT 41
COLLEGES AND UNIVERSITIES
Earl F. Cheit

FINANCING MEDICAL EDUCATION:
AN ANALYSIS OF ALTERNATIVE POLICIES
AND MECHANISMS
Rashi Fein and Gerald I. Weber

HIGHER EDUCATION IN NINE COUNTRIES:
A COMPARATIVE STUDY OF COLLEGES AND
UNIVERSITIES ABROAD
*Barbara B. Burn, Philip G. Altbach, Clark Kerr,
and James A. Perkins*

BRIDGES TO UNDERSTANDING:
INTERNATIONAL PROGRAMS OF AMERICAN
COLLEGES AND UNIVERSITIES
Irwin T. Sanders and Jennifer C. Ward

GRADUATE AND PROFESSIONAL EDUCATION,
1980:
A SURVEY OF INSTITUTIONAL PLANS
Lewis B. Mayhew

THE AMERICAN COLLEGE AND AMERICAN
CULTURE:
SOCIALIZATION AS A FUNCTION OF HIGHER
EDUCATION
Oscar Handlin and Mary F. Handlin

RECENT ALUMNI AND HIGHER EDUCATION:
A SURVEY OF COLLEGE GRADUATES
Joe L. Spaeth and Andrew M. Greeley

CHANGE IN EDUCATIONAL POLICY:
SELF-STUDIES IN SELECTED COLLEGES AND
UNIVERSITIES
Dwight R. Ladd

STATE OFFICIALS AND HIGHER EDUCATION:
A SURVEY OF THE OPINIONS AND
EXPECTATIONS OF POLICY MAKERS IN NINE
STATES
Heinz Eulau and Harold Quinley

ACADEMIC DEGREE STRUCTURES:
INNOVATIVE APPROACHES
PRINCIPLES OF REFORM IN DEGREE
STRUCTURES IN THE UNITED STATES
Stephen H. Spurr

COLLEGES OF THE FORGOTTEN AMERICANS:
A PROFILE OF STATE COLLEGES AND
REGIONAL UNIVERSITIES
E. Alden Dunham

FROM BACKWATER TO MAINSTREAM:
A PROFILE OF CATHOLIC HIGHER
EDUCATION
Andrew M. Greeley

THE ECONOMICS OF THE MAJOR PRIVATE
UNIVERSITIES
William G. Bowen
(Out of print, but available from University Microfilms.)

THE FINANCE OF HIGHER EDUCATION
Howard R. Bowen
(Out of print, but available from University Microfilms.)

ALTERNATIVE METHODS OF FEDERAL
FUNDING FOR HIGHER EDUCATION
Ron Wolk
(Out of print, but available from University Microfilms.)

INVENTORY OF CURRENT RESEARCH ON
HIGHER EDUCATION 1968
Dale M. Heckman and Warren Bryan Martin
(Out of print, but available from University Microfilms.)

*The following technical reports are available from the Carnegie Commission on Higher Education, 1947
Center Street, Berkeley, California 94704.*

RESOURCE USE IN HIGHER EDUCATION:
TRENDS IN OUTPUT AND INPUTS, 1930–1967
June O'Neill

TRENDS AND PROJECTIONS OF PHYSICIANS
IN THE UNITED STATES 1967–2002
Mark S. Blumberg

MAY 1970:
THE CAMPUS AFTERMATH OF CAMBODIA
AND KENT STATE
Richard E. Peterson and John A. Bilorusky

MENTAL ABILITY AND HIGHER EDUCATIONAL
ATTAINMENT IN THE 20TH CENTURY
Paul Taubman and Terence Wales

AMERICAN COLLEGE AND UNIVERSITY
ENROLLMENT TRENDS IN 1971
Richard E. Peterson

PAPERS ON EFFICIENCY IN THE
MANAGEMENT OF HIGHER EDUCATION
*Alexander M. Mood, Colin Bell,
Lawrence Bogard, Helen Brownlee,
and Joseph McCloskey*

ACCELERATED PROGRAMS OF MEDICAL EDUCATION, by Mark S. Blumberg, reprinted from JOURNAL OF MEDICAL EDUCATION, vol. 46, no. 8, August 1971.*

SCIENTIFIC MANPOWER FOR 1970–1985, by Allan M. Cartter, reprinted from SCIENCE, vol. 172, no. 3979, pp. 132–140, April 9, 1971.

A NEW METHOD OF MEASURING STATES' HIGHER EDUCATION BURDEN, by Neil Timm, reprinted from THE JOURNAL OF HIGHER EDUCATION, vol. 42, no. 1, pp. 27–33, January 1971.*

REGENT WATCHING, by Earl F. Cheit, reprinted from AGB REPORTS, vol. 13, no. 6, pp. 4–13, March 1971.

COLLEGE GENERATIONS—FROM THE 1930s TO THE 1960s by Seymour M. Lipset and Everett C. Ladd, Jr., reprinted from THE PUBLIC INTEREST, no. 25, Summer 1971.

AMERICAN SOCIAL SCIENTISTS AND THE GROWTH OF CAMPUS POLITICAL ACTIVISM IN THE 1960s, by Everett C. Ladd, Jr., and Seymour M. Lipset, reprinted from SOCIAL SCIENCES INFORMATION, vol. 10, no. 2, April 1971.

THE POLITICS OF AMERICAN POLITICAL SCIENTISTS, by Everett C. Ladd, Jr., and Seymour M. Lipset, reprinted from PS, vol. 4, no. 2, Spring 1971.*

THE DIVIDED PROFESSORIATE, by Seymour M. Lipset and Everett C. Ladd, Jr., reprinted from CHANGE, vol. 3, no. 3, pp. 54–60, May 1971.*

JEWISH ACADEMICS IN THE UNITED STATES: THEIR ACHIEVEMENTS, CULTURE AND POLITICS, by Seymour M. Lipset and Everett C. Ladd, Jr., reprinted from AMERICAN JEWISH YEAR BOOK, 1971.

THE UNHOLY ALLIANCE AGAINST THE CAMPUS, by Kenneth Keniston and Michael Lerner, reprinted from NEW YORK TIMES MAGAZINE, November 8, 1970 .

PRECARIOUS PROFESSORS: NEW PATTERNS OF REPRESENTATION, by Joseph W. Garbarino, reprinted from INDUSTRIAL RELATIONS, vol. 10, no. 1, February 1971.*

. . . AND WHAT PROFESSORS THINK: ABOUT STUDENT PROTEST AND MANNERS, MORALS, POLITICS, AND CHAOS ON THE CAMPUS, by Seymour Martin Lipset and Everett C. Ladd, Jr., reprinted from PSYCHOLOGY TODAY, November 1970.*

DEMAND AND SUPPLY IN U.S. HIGHER EDUCATION: A PROGRESS REPORT, by Roy Radner and Leonard S. Miller, reprinted from AMERICAN ECONOMIC REVIEW, May 1970.*

RESOURCES FOR HIGHER EDUCATION: AN ECONOMIST'S VIEW, by Theodore W. Schultz, reprinted from JOURNAL OF POLITICAL ECONOMY, vol. 76, no. 3, University of Chicago, May/June 1968.*

INDUSTRIAL RELATIONS AND UNIVERSITY RELATIONS, *by Clark Kerr, reprinted from* PRO-
CEEDINGS OF THE 21ST ANNUAL WINTER MEETING OF THE INDUSTRIAL RELATIONS RESEARCH
ASSOCIATION, *pp. 15–25.**

NEW CHALLENGES TO THE COLLEGE AND UNIVERSITY, *by Clark Kerr, reprinted from Kermit
Gordon (ed.),* AGENDA FOR THE NATION, *The Brookings Institution, Washington, D.C.,
1968.**

PRESIDENTIAL DISCONTENT, *by Clark Kerr, reprinted from David C. Nichols (ed.),* PER-
SPECTIVES ON CAMPUS TENSIONS: PAPERS PREPARED FOR THE SPECIAL COMMITTEE ON CAMPUS
TENSIONS, *American Council on Education, Washington, D.C., September 1970.**

STUDENT PROTEST—AN INSTITUTIONAL AND NATIONAL PROFILE, *by Harold Hodgkinson,
reprinted from* THE RECORD, *vol. 71, no. 4, May 1970.**

WHAT'S BUGGING THE STUDENTS?, *by Kenneth Keniston, reprinted from* EDUCATIONAL
RECORD, *American Council on Education, Washington, D.C., Spring 1970.**

THE POLITICS OF ACADEMIA, *by Seymour Martin Lipset, reprinted from David C. Nichols
(ed.),* PERSPECTIVES ON CAMPUS TENSIONS: PAPERS PREPARED FOR THE SPECIAL COMMITTEE
ON CAMPUS TENSIONS, *American Council on Education, Washington, D.C., September
1970.**

INTERNATIONAL PROGRAMS OF U.S. COLLEGES AND UNIVERSITIES: PRIORITIES FOR THE SEVEN-
TIES, *by James A. Perkins, reprinted by permission of the International Council for Educational Development, Occasional Paper no. 1, July 1971.*

FACULTY UNIONISM: FROM THEORY TO PRACTICE, *by Joseph W. Garbarino, reprinted from*
INDUSTRIAL RELATIONS, *vol. 11, no. 1, pp. 1–17, February 1972.*

MORE FOR LESS: HIGHER EDUCATION'S NEW PRIORITY, *by Virginia B. Smith, reprinted from*
UNIVERSAL HIGHER EDUCATION: COSTS AND BENEFITS, *American Council on Education,
Washington, D.C., 1971.*

ACADEMIA AND POLITICS IN AMERICA, *by Seymour M. Lipset, reprinted from Thomas J.
Nossiter (ed.),* IMAGINATION AND PRECISION IN THE SOCIAL SCIENCES, *pp. 211–289, Faber
and Faber, London, 1972.*

POLITICS OF ACADEMIC NATURAL SCIENTISTS AND ENGINEERS, *by Everett C. Ladd, Jr., and
Seymour M. Lipset, reprinted from* SCIENCE, *vol. 176, no. 4039, pp. 1091–1100, June 9,
1972.*

THE INTELLECTUAL AS CRITIC AND REBEL: WITH SPECIAL REFERENCE TO THE UNITED STATES
AND THE SOVIET UNION, *by Seymour M. Lipset and Richard B. Dobson, reprinted from*
DAEDALUS, *vol. 101, no. 3, pp. 137–198, Summer 1972.*

**The Commission's stock of this reprint has been exhausted.*